WRT 150

A Guide to First-Year Writing at Grand Valley State University

10th Edition
2011-12

Edited by
Dauvan Mulally

Grand Valley State University
Allendale, Michigan

TAPESTRY PRESS, LTD.
Littleton, MA 01460

Printed in the United States of America

ISBN 978-1-59830-507-4

Contents

First-Year Writing at Grand Valley

Introduction

Welcome to the Department of Writing's first-year writing program at Grand Valley State University. Our courses improve your writing, critical thinking, and information literacy skills. In this course, you will gain abilities that will carry over into the rest of your university experience, and beyond. The goal of this book, A Guide to First-Year Writing at Grand Valley State University, is just that—to guide you in your writing endeavors. From here on, we will just call this book the Guide. As a community of writers, we have worked to create a Guide that invites you into our community and celebrates student writing at all stages. We hope you will make extensive use of this Guide, both in class and on your own, to succeed in our required first-year writing course, Writing 150 ("WRT 150" in the Grand Valley catalog).

Our Department of Writing strives to create a consistent program for all students who take WRT 150. Our professors teach WRT 150 using their own preferred teaching methods, but important elements remain consistent across all sections. We have standardized foundational elements like course objectives, grading criteria, grading methods, and departmental policies—all of which you will find explained in this book. Each semester every WRT 150 teacher meets once a week with other teachers to discuss these course goals and expectations as they apply to particular students' papers. At the end of the term, these groups of teachers read final portfolios of the work that students produce in WRT 150 and assign each portfolio a grade. As a result, at Grand Valley, you can compare your grade at the end of your first-year writing experience fairly with the grade of every other student on campus who has taken WRT 150.

This Guide tells you more about our shared course expectations for WRT 150. At the beginning, we provide brief descriptions of the other courses that you might take before taking WRT 150, just in case you wish to reconsider your choice of the right place to start your college writing experience. Then we provide a much more detailed guide to WRT 150. First, we provide course policies. Next, to help you understand how to prepare your work for portfolio grading, we include our WRT 150 portfolio submission guidelines. Then we provide descriptions of our grading standards—the same descriptions that we use when we grade your portfolios. After the grading descriptions, we offer further information about keys to success in WRT 150. We also provide information about support that we offer to help you succeed.

After that discussion, we include several A level portfolios from last year's WRT 150 students to guide your revisions and spur classroom discussion of the grading expectations. Finally, we also include effective student writing from a range of academic courses around campus.

Other Course Options

As you know by now, you decide which writing course you should take first at Grand Valley, after considering information about our departmental requirements and consulting with advisors during orientation. You have these three choices:

- ESL 098 is for second-language students making a transition to standard written English.
- WRT 098 is for students who need more practice and instruction to develop fluency and fullness in their writing.
- WRT 150 is for students who write fluently and are ready to begin college-level academic writing, including writing with sources.

About 85 percent of students who enter Grand Valley place themselves into WRT 150—a four-credit course designed to prepare you for writing in your college classes. If you are reading this Guide, you have already made that choice. Just in case you would like to consider your choice one more time, here are brief descriptions of your other options. If you have doubts about the course you have chosen, talk about your concerns with your professor as soon as possible. Your professor may also assign a quick writing task during the first week of the course, in part to help you make that decision.

ESL 098

Specialists in second language learning teach ESL 098, offered by the Department of English. It is the best starting place for students for whom English language provides more difficulty than writing itself. In particular, students who are highly successful writers in another language but who have difficulty writing in English should take ESL 098 rather than WRT 098.

WRT 098

WRT 098 focuses on raising students' confidence in their writing, assisting them in gaining agency and control over their writing and education, and encouraging them to value a lifelong engagement with writing and reading. Students write to learn as well as to communicate, and they learn more about the practice of writing, particularly writing in college. The course invites spontaneity and discovery, seeking to develop in students the kinds of habits and writing strategies that will enable them to succeed in WRT 150 and beyond.

WRT 098 emphasizes immersion, invention, and revision. Students write continually, generating new drafts all semester long. Students learn invention strategies to get papers started, learn to keep the writing process going to produce a substantial volume of writing, and develop positive attitudes toward writing. Revision, by which we mean truly re-seeing and re-imagining each new draft, helps students develop the habits by which highly effective writers continue to improve the quality of their writing before turning to final editing. WRT 098 features peer workshop groups led by trained writing consultants from The Fred Meijer Center for Writing (the "Writing Center"), so that students learn not only the benefits of seeking assistance from the Writing Center but also the value of thoughtful peer review.

Students in WRT 098 receive a preliminary introduction to college-level research skills, using the Internet and the more advanced research materials available through Grand Valley's library and the library's online resources. WRT 098 also introduces students to using computers in ways that WRT 150 will require. Students who need more help with these more technical aspects of college writing may also want to start in WRT 098.

Overview of WRT 150

As the single writing course required of all Grand Valley students, WRT 150 focuses on academic writing, including writing informed by scholarly research. Teachers assume that you are ready to read, summarize, and analyze a wide variety of college-level published material. They also assume that you have experience with narrative, descriptive, and argumentative writing. In most WRT 150 classes, you first write four or five papers, at least one of which integrates material from highly credible sources that you find in the course of doing significant academic research. In most cases, these papers will be four to ten pages long in normal academic format. From among these papers, you will pick three, including at least one that demonstrates your research skills and strategies, to include in your final portfolio for grading. Then, you will spend a considerable amount of time revising and improving your three portfolio papers.

In WRT 150, you encounter challenging reading material—whether you find it in assigned readings or in your own research materials—and you practice discussing, summarizing, and analyzing that material. You also work on developing writing processes that can help you complete new kinds of writing tasks and rise to new levels of writing ability—processes that move effectively from prewriting, inventing, planning, and drafting to revising, consulting, editing, and finishing.

In most sections, half of your WRT 150 class meetings take place in a computer classroom. Each computer is connected to the Internet and the Grand Valley network. The Grand Valley network includes personal storage space on the campus server and special access to research sources maintained by Grand Valley's library system. WRT 150 teachers assume that you have a basic familiarity with computers, word processors, web browsers, and email.

By the end of WRT 150, as an experienced college writer you should be able to:

Prewrite, Invent, and Plan

- Read and understand material written for college audiences.
- Develop clearly focused written summaries, analyses, and paraphrases that demonstrate an understanding of the material you have read.
- Develop ideas using a variety of prewriting techniques, which may include brainstorming, freewriting, journal-keeping, consulting with others, conducting library research, and analyzing your audiences.

Revise, Develop, and Shape

- Develop writing from early, writer-oriented drafts to later, reader-oriented drafts.
- Produce effective writing for a variety of purposes, such as narrating, explaining, exploring, and persuading.
- Demonstrate the ability to focus your writing on supportable themes, claims, or theories.
- Support your focus using well-selected details that are suggestive, accurate, and relevant.
- Consult with peer reviewers and other readers to assess the further needs of your drafts.
- Revise writing with particular audiences in mind, including academic audiences.
- Conduct effective, significant scholarly research.
- Integrate facts and opinions from a variety of sources into your own writing.

Refine, Edit, and Finish

- Include words, facts, and ideas from research sources in ways that fully credit the original source and avoid plagiarism.
- Control the main features of a specific documentation style (like MLA or APA).
- Refine your sentence structures to produce an effective style and voice.
- Edit writing so that academic audiences can read the writing without having their attention and understanding diverted by problems in grammar, spelling, punctuation, and format.

In addition to requiring WRT 150, Grand Valley supports the development of your writing ability in other courses. Many General Education courses focus on developing your writing in specific academic areas. You do not need to finish WRT 150 before taking those classes. They work along with WRT 150 to develop your writing foundation. After building that foundation, you will take two courses in disciplines of interest to you specifically designated as Supplemental Writing Skills courses. You may also take further writing courses, and many of your college courses will involve extensive writing. Thus, WRT 150 is not the end of your college writing instruction. Instead, it seeks to supply you with an important foundation for further development.

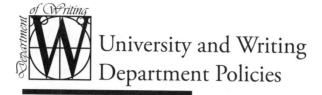

University and Writing Department Policies

WRT 150 Course Policies

WRT 150 sections can have many differences in terms of assignments, daily routines, and instruction. We want all teachers to teach in the ways that best suit their abilities and the needs of their particular students. Nevertheless, as part of our effort to ensure consistency across sections, all WRT 150 teachers adhere to the following university and departmental policies.

Required Passing Grade

You must pass WRT 150 with a grade of C or better (above C-) to satisfy Grand Valley's Writing Skills Requirement. If you do not receive a grade of C or better, you will need to take WRT 150 again.

Learning or Physical Disabilities

If you have any special needs because of learning, physical, or any other disabilities, please contact Disability Support Services at 616-331-2490. Any student needing academic accommodations beyond those given to the entire class needs to request assistance from DSS. Writing faculty work with DSS to accommodate students' special needs and devise a plan that is fair to all students. Furthermore, if you have a disability and think you will need assistance evacuating a classroom and/or building in an emergency situation, please make your teacher and DSS aware so that Grand Valley can develop a plan to assist you.

Attendance

Regular, timely, and full attendance is required to succeed in WRT 150. According to the Grand Valley catalog, teachers may fail students for excessive absences. In WRT 150, missing class more than four times constitutes excessive absences, and can be grounds for failing the course. Tardiness, leaving class while it is in session, and coming unprepared may also count as an absence or partial absence according to your teacher's policies. Your teacher should send you an email warning after the fourth absence. If you miss class or come unprepared after such a warning, you will be ineligible to submit a final portfolio for the course, which means you will fail. Excessive absence itself is the grounds for failure, so that lack of warning does not excuse your absences. The warning simply provides additional clarity.

WRT 150 Goals

By the end of WRT 150, your final portfolio should demonstrate that you have achieved the program's goals and can perform each of these tasks:

Content and Development:
- Offer readers a clear purpose for reading.
- Maintain a single focus throughout the entire paper.
- Present ideas and descriptions that engage a college-level audience in your discussion.
- Conduct college-level research to find credible source material for a variety of purposes.
- Present a claim or focus that is developed with discussion, details, and examples, including graphics when useful.
- Discover and integrate sufficient material from outside sources to demonstrate your abilities in college level writing, research, and thinking.

Organization:
- Establish an overall pattern for a paper to follow.
- Progress from one point, idea, or scene to another in a coherent, logical way.
- Construct paragraphs that are generally well-organized within the overall pattern of a paper.
- Lead readers through the order of your discussion in obvious and helpful ways.

Style:
- Craft sentences with purposefully chosen words and phrases.
- Structure sentences effectively to be clear, logical, and readable
- Use a variety of sentence structures for good reasons.
- Maintain an overall voice in each paper that is appropriate for its purpose, genre, and audiences.

Mechanics:

- Adopt a format that is acceptable and appropriate for academic writing.
- Refer to outside sources that are introduced, integrated, and documented.
- Attend carefully to grammar, spelling, punctuation, and usage in final, edited writing.
- Use with care a standard academic style guide, such as the MLA or APA style guides.

WRT 150 Portfolio Guidelines

Portfolio Grading

We determine all final grades in WRT 150 by evaluating a final portfolio containing three of your papers. Your own teacher's portfolio grading group grades your portfolio. We use this method so that our grading can be as fair and accurate as possible. Our teachers work very hard to make sure that this method gives you the best and fairest result.

Your teacher's portfolio grading group (usually four to six teachers) reads and discusses samples of writing from your class throughout the semester to agree about standards for A, B, C, and D papers. Their standards begin with those established by the Writing Department and set forth more specifically further on in this Guide, at pages 12-20. Through their discussions, the groups work to fit those standards more specifically to your assignments and the work done by your class.

At the end of the semester, your teacher and one other teacher from the portfolio grading group will read and grade your portfolio. If they disagree about the grade, a third teacher in that group reads your portfolio and decides which reader, your teacher or the other teacher, has come closest to the standards that the portfolio group has agreed upon during the semester. Agreement between two or more teachers determines your letter grade in the class. For example, if your portfolio receives a B from the first two readers, you receive a B on your portfolio. If your portfolio receives an A from one reader, a B from another, and an A from a third reader, you receive an A on your portfolio. By using this method, we seek to arrive at a "community" grade based on the quality of your writing rather than a grade based solely on one teacher's preferences or on your teacher's personal opinion of you.

Once the portfolio grading group arrives at a letter grade, your teacher also has the option of adding a "plus" or "minus" to the final letter grade based on other aspects of your work, such as attendance, class participation, effective peer-review, and completion of reading assignments. Teachers should not raise or lower your grade any further than a plus or minus, which ensures the highest degree of fairness based on the quality of your work.

The portfolios are graded after class is over, and students should keep their own copies of papers, so the portfolios are not returned. For those reasons, we do not write comments on the papers or the portfolios. Teachers do often write very brief notes about grades of D so that students receiving this grade may ask about the reasons for that grade.

If you have any questions about the grade that you receive, ask your teacher to discuss your grade with you.

Semester-long Evaluation

The fact that you earn your grade with your final portfolio does not mean that the evaluation of your writing should be a mystery. First, you should learn how to apply the grading criteria to your own writing. Your teacher should read your writing throughout the semester and respond to it with comments, personal conferences, and suggestions for revision. Many teachers will have you read, comment on, and evaluate other students' work. For most students, a grade is not necessary for early drafts because the proper focus is on what the paper could become, not on what it is. But if you want a grade on an assignment and your teacher has not given one, just ask. Teachers will be able to tell you where they think the paper falls within the range of A to D. Your teacher will probably tell you what the portfolio group has been saying about writing like yours.

Nevertheless, it is important to remember that all grade estimates—whether they are by you, your teacher, your classmates, or your Aunt Lou—are just that: estimates. Ultimately, the grade will depend on the entire portfolio in its final form, something nobody will be able to review carefully until the end of the term. Mainly what you need to do is just keep on working. If the teacher says your paper is probably a low B or a C, your next question should be: "What could I work on in this paper that would improve it?" Improve your research and your writing until the very last day, and you will receive the best grade available to you. Meanwhile, you should also seek to improve your own judgment of your own grade, using the grading criteria. The most successful and satisfied WRT 150 students do not need the teacher to tell them what grade they are getting; they already have a fairly good idea themselves.

Midterm Evaluation

Grand Valley requires midterm grade reports for first-year students and some upper-level students. Midterm grades are available on the web but not recorded on your official transcript. Midterm grades in WRT 150 can only assess the overall quality of your work in the class up to that point and your prospects for doing better. Such assessments have no direct bearing on your final grade because we base WRT 150 grades on the quality of your writing at the end of the term, as determined by portfolio grading. For a full explanation of your midterm grade, please consult with your teacher.

Your Final Portfolio

Evaluation Procedures

Many professionals use portfolios to show other people what they are capable of producing. Your WRT 150 portfolio represents your own end-of-semester writing capabilities. The portfolio includes three fully revised and polished papers, including at least one that integrates outside sources and accurately credits the ideas and language drawn from those sources. Together, these three pieces of writing produce the bulk of your final course grade.

The three papers in your portfolio represent your abilities as a college-level academic writer, so you should select them with care. For example, you probably do not want three very short papers, since that would fail to show your ability to write a longer paper. Ask your teacher and peer reviewers about your selections if you are not sure. Your teacher and the other students should help you make good choices about what goes in the final portfolio. Also, read the full portfolios published in this book, and, together with your teacher and classmates, try to generalize from them what constitutes a strong WRT 150 portfolio.

As explained earlier in this Guide, your WRT 150 portfolio is read and evaluated by at least two members of a group of teachers, including your own professor, that meets regularly throughout the term to discuss grading criteria and expectations. Your readers supply one grade per portfolio; that is, they do not grade the individual papers, but rather the entire portfolio. Your first priority should be to include your best writing, but your second priority should be to demonstrate your ability to perform a range of academic writing tasks. Of course, as part of that range of academic writing tasks, you must demonstrate that you can conduct responsible academic research and integrate a variety of reputable sources into your writing.

So that your teacher has time to check all work for any problems, we strictly enforce your teachers' requirements for turning in earlier versions of work that you intend to place in your portfolio. All papers in your portfolio must have been assigned for the class and seen by your teacher in draft form before final submission.

Submission Guidelines

Your final portfolio will consist of three final papers, each individually stapled. Papers should be printed on a letter-quality printer. If your teacher gives no special instructions, follow these further guidelines. Margins should be one inch all the way around the page and lines should be double-spaced. Fonts should be common or default types (Arial, Calibri, Times New Roman, etc.), and the point-size should be close to standard typeface (11 or 12 points). If your teacher has special instructions for the form or format of your papers, the portfolio grading groups will honor those instructions.

In addition to requiring you to submit earlier drafts, your teacher is entitled to set further requirements before your portfolio will be eligible for grading. Common requirements are that you attend class regularly, submit papers on time in response to individual assignments, use particular formats, or submit papers at a specific length or level of editing care. If you do not meet your teacher's specific requirements, your teacher may refuse to submit your portfolio for grading, in which case you will fail the course. Such requirements should be set out clearly in your teacher's syllabus, assignments, or other written instructions to which the syllabus refers.

Submit your papers in a standard manila file folder with your first initial, last name, and section clearly written on the filing tab. Your portfolio is due to your teacher by the end of the last class before finals week, unless your teacher's syllabus sets a different deadline. If your portfolio is late, you may fail the course.

The portfolio grading groups do not comment on portfolios except for brief notes on D portfolios, so portfolios are not returned. You should keep copies of your work and wait for grade reports to see your course grades. If there are questions about your grade, you should speak with your teacher. The Department may keep your portfolio and use it for internal studies of our teaching and its results, but we will not publish the contents of your writing without your permission. Most teachers recycle the paper versions of your documents after the end of the semester following the one when you turned in the portfolio.

Evaluation Criteria—Characteristics of A, B, C, and D Papers

We provide the general characteristics of A, B, and C portfolios for you here so that you can identify precisely how your work is evaluated. Characteristics that cause portfolios to fall below the standard for a passing grade are presented as characteristics of D papers. Factors that can cause you to receive an F for the course are listed at the end of the grading criteria. Your teacher, with the help of the teacher's portfolio grading group, will develop more specific understandings of these criteria to apply to your exact assignments and portfolios; in doing so, however, all of them will be seeking to apply the general characteristics below accurately and fairly to your work.

Our approach does mean that we do not reward effort unless it produces results. We want to ensure that what counts as A, B, C, D, or F will be roughly the same for every student in every section, based on achievement.

Characteristics of A Papers

Content and Research

- The portfolio consistently engages the interest of intelligent and sophisticated college-level readers.
- Papers effectively address and engage their likely and intended audiences.
- Papers succeed at accomplishing challenging purposes.
- Each paper maintains a consistent focus on the main claim or goal for the paper.
- Each paper develops its focus with significant and interesting discussion, details, and examples, including graphics when useful.
- The portfolio clearly demonstrates the writer's information literacy and ability to use college-level academic research as a significant means to develop the writer's ideas.
- The portfolio clearly demonstrates the writer's ability to introduce and integrate material from relevant outside sources in ways that advance the purposes for the writing and meet the expectations of intelligent and sophisticated college-level readers.

Organization

- Titles and opening sections of papers inform readers appropriately of the topic, purpose, and focus of the paper in ways that motivate readers to look forward to reading further.
- Paragraphs are purposefully organized and substantially developed with supporting evidence, examples, and reasoning.
- Paragraphs break information into parts that contribute to a greater understanding of the whole.
- Readers can easily see how the order in which information appears supports the focus and purpose of the papers.
- The papers lead readers through the order of the discussion in ways that are explicit, clear, and purposeful, including effective transition devices when needed.
- Readers can see a meaningful pattern in the order of the information as a whole.
- Closing sections give readers a satisfied sense that the purpose of the writing has been achieved.

Style

- Word choice is precise, interesting, and appropriate to the writing task and audience.
- Language is mature and purposefully controlled.
- Sentences are clear, logical, enjoyable, and easily understood by college-level readers.
- Sentences often make active statements and use efficient and effective modification.
- Sentence structure varies according to the content, purpose, and audience.
- A consistent voice complements the papers' purposes, fits their genres, and appeals to their likely and intended readers.
- Information and quotations from sources are integrated skillfully into the writer's own sentences and paragraphs.

Mechanics

- Format is consistent with the detailed requirements of an applicable style guide, such as the MLA or APA style guides.
- References to outside sources are cited and documented according to the appropriate style guide carefully enough that readers can easily identify the sources that have been quoted or referenced.
- Problems in grammar, spelling, punctuation, or usage do not interfere with communication.
- Editing shows respectful and effective attention to the desire of readers to read without being interrupted by unexpected errors or problems with documentation and format.

Characteristics of B Papers

Content and Research

- The portfolio connects with the interest of intelligent and sophisticated college-level readers.
- Papers clearly address the expectations of their likely and intended audiences.
- Papers accomplish interesting purposes or make strong attempts to accomplish challenging purposes.
- Each paper maintains a consistent, single focus.
- Each paper develops a focus with fitting and relevant discussions, details, and examples, including graphics when useful.
- The portfolio demonstrates the writer's ability to use college-level academic research clearly and purposefully to develop the writer's ideas and improve the papers in which research is used.
- The portfolio demonstrates the writer's ability to introduce and integrate material from relevant outside sources in ways that enhance the accomplishment of goals and purposes.

Organization

- Titles and opening sections of papers are well-chosen and appropriate to the topic and focus of the papers.
- Paragraphs are clearly organized and adequately developed with supporting evidence, examples, and reasoning, though some paragraphs may lack richness of detail or evidence.
- Paragraphs break information into parts that make sense and assist effective reading.
- Readers can identify the focus of each paper and follow it through the entire discussion.
- Readers can identify how the order in which information appears supports the focus and purpose of the papers.
- Overall patterns in the order of presentation make sense.
- Transitions between and within paragraphs advance the writer's ideas.
- Closing sections give readers a clear sense that the writer is ending the discussion at a good place.

Style

- Word choice is generally appropriate to the writing task and audience.
- Language is generally mature and purposefully controlled.
- Sentences are generally clear, logical, and readable.
- Sentences typically make active statements, extended by efficient and effective modification.
- Sentences vary in structure and only occasionally are choppy, rambling, or repetitive.
- The voice in each paper is consistent and appropriate for the writer's purpose and the audience.
- Information and quotations from sources make sense within the writer's own sentences and paragraphs.

Mechanics

- Format is appropriate and generally follows the requirements of an assigned style guide, such as the MLA or APA style guides.
- References to outside sources are cited and documented according to the appropriate style guide carefully enough that readers can determine when source material has been used and find the sources.
- Problems in grammar, spelling, punctuation, or usage rarely interfere with communication.
- Editing shows diligent and informed attention to the desire of readers to read without being interrupted by unexpected errors.

Characteristics of C Papers

Content and Research

- The portfolio makes sense to intelligent and sophisticated college-level readers, though it may not consistently hold their interest.
- The portfolio presents ideas and descriptions with readers in mind.
- Papers appear to aim at accomplishing purposes.
- Each paper generally maintains a single focus, though the focus may be on a topic or an event rather than an idea, claim or goal.
- Each paper generally develops a focus with details, examples, and discussions, including graphics when useful.
- The portfolio demonstrates the writer's ability to use relevant college-level academic research as a means to develop a topic.
- The portfolio demonstrates the writer's ability to include material from outside sources within the general requirements of an applicable style guide.

Organization

- Titles and openings generally match the topic and focus.
- Paragraphs make sense and usually use some evidence or detailed examples to support points.
- Papers generally establish an overall organizational pattern for readers to follow.
- Each paper develops a basic focus, with few paragraphs appearing to be out of sequence or off-track.
- Transitions from one section and idea to another are evident and make sense.

Style

- Most words appear to be well chosen and fit the purpose and audience for the particular paper.
- Most of the time sentences are not short and choppy, long and rambling, or vague and wordy.
- Sentences are generally readable and make sense.
- Sentences sometimes feature the efficient and effective uses of modifying clauses and phrases.

- The writer's voice is consistent and appropriate, usually fitting the writer's purpose, genre, and audience.
- Information and quotations from sources is clearly presented as source material.

Mechanics

- Format choices are generally appropriate for the purposes of the papers.
- References to outside sources are generally cited and documented, if not always in the appropriate style; readers can determine when source material has been quoted or referenced, and instances of unreferenced source material are few, unimportant, and clearly not intentional.
- Mistakes in grammar, spelling, punctuation, or usage do not generally interfere with either the writer's credibility or the reader's ability to read the text easily.
- Editing shows adequate attention to the desire of readers to read without being interrupted by unexpected errors.

D Portfolios

Regardless of writing ability, portfolios will receive the grade of D if, as a whole, the portfolio fails to demonstrate that the student understands how to conduct college-level research as well as how to integrate the results of such research into purposeful writing without committing plagiarism. Otherwise, D portfolios rarely have similar characteristics. The lists below present the danger signals that help predict when a portfolio does not demonstrate competence. The main key to avoiding a D is to meet the criteria for at least a C.

Content & Research

- Topics, purposes, claims, or focuses are so simplistic and obvious that they do not engage the interest of college-educated readers.
- Papers have no apparent and appropriate audiences.
- Papers have no clear purposes.
- At least one paper is clearly fictional.
- Papers lack a single focus.
- Ideas are stated, but they are not developed with details, examples, and discussions.
- Language or material from sources are consistently presented in ways that are very hard to follow.
- Unintentional, careless misuse of source material would amount to plagiarism had it been intentional.
- The portfolio shows weak research and information literacy abilities, such as the use of very few sources, little variety of sources, or little obvious effort to conduct scholarly or professional research.
- Sources do not support and may even contradict the views that the writer attributes to them.

Organization

- Openings and endings are overly general, missing, or misleading.
- Readers cannot readily see the focus of the papers.
- Paragraphs frequently seem unrelated to each other or repetitive.
- Paragraphs do not develop logically from start to finish, or they break in illogical places.
- Paragraphs often end without developing broad, general statements

with evidence and reasoning.

- Transitions between and within paragraphs are weak, ineffective, or misleading.
- The papers do not establish clear patterns for readers to follow.

Style

- Sentences often are short and choppy, long and rambling, or vague and wordy.
- Disordered sentence parts, poor phrasing, and poor word choices make reading difficult.
- Sentences often disregard the normal rules of standard written English in ways that make ideas hard to understand.
- The voice often appears inappropriate for the writer's purpose, genre, and audience.

Mechanics

- Format, including any use of graphics, is extremely careless or entirely disregards the basic requirements of applicable style guides.
- Language or material from outside sources is not clearly cited.
- Documentation style is generally wrong according to the assigned style guide, often in ways that interfere with readers' abilities to find the source material and locate the referenced portions of the sources.
- Instances of misused source material show careless inattention to important requirements for quoting, paraphrasing, and citing, raising questions of possible plagiarism.
- Many errors in spelling, grammar, punctuation, word choice, and usage make reading difficult, or they strongly limit the writer's credibility.

F Grades

The grade of F in WRT 150 is reserved for the following circumstances:

- The student did not turn in a portfolio by the last day of class (or the due date set by the teacher's syllabus, if the teacher chooses another due date).
- The portfolio did not have three papers in it that qualified for the portfolio under this Guide and the teacher's syllabus.
- The student violated course polices set by this Guide or the teacher's syllabus (for example, an attendance policy), if the information made clear that the violation would result in a grade of F.
- The student violated other policies of Grand Valley State University that clearly state that the violation could result in a grade of F.
- The student clearly committed plagiarism, as described by Grand Valley's Student Code, this Guide, and the teacher's syllabus.
- The portfolio clearly demonstrates a complete indifference to earning any higher grade.

Grade Appeals

If for any reason you need to appeal your final grade, please consult the Student Code for the applicable procedures. Your first contact should be with the teacher of your class. Appeals from your teacher's decision to the Department of Writing should be directed to Keith Rhodes, the Director of WRT 150, and be supported by a written appeal explaining how your portfolio displays the characteristics of the grade that you are seeking. Appeals to the Director of WRT 150 may be forwarded by e-mail at rhodekei@gvsu.edu or delivered to the Department of Writing directed to the attention of the Director of WRT 150.

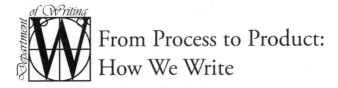

From Process to Product: How We Write

Writing as a Process

When we think of writers, we might imagine people who possess some magical talent that allows them to sit down and instantly put their thoughts into writing. But after observing experienced writers working from start to finish through real writing projects, researchers have concluded that expert writers do not simply sit down and "put it in writing" in one magical step. Rather, expert writers work through a complex series of steps, or "process." Different writers follow different steps depending on their needs and personal preferences, but in general expert writers experience writing as a process that unfolds over time, not as a "one and done" burst of inspiration.

For instance, when faced with the need to communicate to an audience, expert writers begin by exploring their own knowledge, feelings, and beliefs and often consult the knowledge, feelings, and beliefs of others, searching for something specific to say. Then they explore their communication options—the various forms available to them—before sketching out, reconsidering, revising, and polishing their message, making sure they are sensitive to their readers. Often, at several points during the writing process, expert writers ask friends or peers—people no more expert than they are, and often less so—to take a look at their drafted material and give advice or feedback. Finally, when satisfied with their efforts, expert writers polish the results and deliver their writing to their intended audience.

The example above illustrates five basic parts of a successful writing process:

- Prewriting and Inventing: generating ideas; forming questions for investigation and constructing a research plan; collecting, evaluating, and managing information; identifying possible subjects, purposes, audiences, and forms;
- Planning and Drafting: trying out ideas and approaches; zeroing in

on a single focus and a single form;

- Consulting: talking with people about preliminary ideas, plans, and drafts; soliciting oral and written feedback from friends and colleagues concerning content, structure, audience appeal, style, and correctness;
- Revising and Shaping: considering additions and deletions; reshaping and refocusing existing material, and editing for style, flow, and obvious error;
- Editing and Finishing: taking authorial responsibility for the final product; editing carefully for correctness and format; and delivering the final product to its intended audience (teacher, relative, client, committee, editor, etc.).

While you will probably have a unique way of going through the steps set out above, at some point all expert writers need to find ways of addressing the concerns of each step effectively. As teachers of WRT 150, we are not merely judges of your writing. In fact, you might best view teachers as coaches whose primary goal is to help you develop processes that you will use for the writing you do in WRT 150, in future Grand Valley classes, and on the job. We help you explore your writing processes through class information, class discussions, stimulating writing assignments, and responses to your writing in progress.

Your teacher will help you explore your writing processes, but you can take control of your own processes by considering the following checklist that we have devised to help you develop expert methods.

Prewriting and Inventing:

- Use a variety of brainstorming techniques to generate, develop, and focus topics.
- Write informally in journals or notebooks as an ongoing writer's activity.
- Use writing as a tool for learning as well as communicating.
- Analyze audience as a method of planning and focusing.
- Consider purpose, style, and form in relation to audience during the planning stages.
- Weigh a variety of form and style options during the planning stages.

- Sequence and initiate your own writing process to suit immediate purposes.
- Generate and select your own methods for developing material.
- Engage in prewriting discussions with your instructor and peers.
- Read as a writer; read published materials critically.
- Write and speak about yourself as a writer.
- Form questions for investigation and construct a research plan.
- Collect, evaluate, and manage information.
- Use basic reference materials (dictionary, encyclopedia, online search engine).
- Use research as a form of generating ideas and planning writing.
- Consider how numerical and graphic information might support your focus and purpose.

Planning and Drafting:

- Translate prewriting activities into drafts.
- Adapt your writing for specific readers, including academic ones.
- Write for broad, public, academic audiences.
- Vary diction and tone according to audience.
- Establish and maintain a focus that has a purpose.
- Maintain a consistent style throughout the different parts.
- Cultivate an appropriate and interesting voice.
- Integrate ideas and information from outside sources.
- Support ideas and observations with details, including numerical and graphic information.
- Use a word processor to capture your writing and save different versions when you make important changes.

Consulting:

- Use feedback from peers.
- Give feedback to peers.
- Engage in revision discussions with your instructor, peers, and writing consultant.
- Survey and integrate readers' needs and interests.
- Write alternate and more fully realized new versions of earlier drafts.
- Work productively in writing groups.

Revising and Shaping:

- Write and use your own evaluations of your drafts.
- Adapt the style and voice of your language to suit your purpose and audience.
- Revise for focus, development, order, structure, balance, and emphasis.
- Align the information and reasoning in the paper with the paper's focus.
- Add, delete, change, or recast material to suit your purposes and readers.
- Establish a clear focus throughout the paper.
- Consider the full variety of readers for whom you might actually be writing.
- Revise paragraphing and sentences for greater clarity and interest.
- Achieve "closure" in later drafts; make sure the product can become a consistent whole work.

Editing and Finishing:

- Proofread all writing intended for public audiences.
- Use your word processor's editing software to help you spot possible areas for improvement.
- Refresh your editing eye and ear by using methods like reading aloud, reading sentences in reverse order, reading as if you were somebody else (like your favorite Uncle or Aunt), or putting the latest draft away for a day or two.
- Use a dictionary and handbook for editing.
- Check your documentation with a guide for your documentation style.
- Check your use of material from sources to be sure you are using source material ethically.

Responding to Peer Writing

While reviewing the written "Process-Skills Checklist" can be instrumental in improving your papers, you will find that spoken feedback can be particularly helpful as well in the drafting process. Therefore, you will play a vital role in this information exchange. By offering valuable feedback on other students' papers, you will increase your ability to think critically about your own writing and at the same time receive valuable feedback to help you improve your paper drafts. As you consider this part of the process, you should avoid closing the door with final negative or positive evaluations on students' papers. If you judge early drafts by saying "your opening is perfect" or "this is already an A paper," you encourage your peers to stop rethinking and rewriting their papers.

Your teacher will probably have many suggestions about how to do successful peer review. Probably the least valuable thing peers can do for each other, at least without specific teacher guidance, is trying to fix each other's sentence errors. Try to ignore even the errors that you see—at least at first—so that you can give readers feedback on their content, organization, and style. After all, those things will probably determine much more of their grade. You may not be an expert on grammar, but you are an expert on what the writing communicated to you. Give the writer the benefit of what you know best.

Information Literacy

As academic writers, we work in a world of information and opinion, so it is very common for us to refer to facts and ideas originally published in other sources, and then to quote and cite those sources in ways that carefully show where we got our information. Educators commonly refer to this ability as "information literacy." We focus on information literacy for three main reasons. First, we want readers to take us seriously because we have done our homework; we have taken the time to find out what the best experts on the subject have already said. Second, we want to give proper credit to those who have already written on the subject; after all, we want credit for our own work, so we afford others the same courtesy. Third, we want our readers to know that credible experts agree with us.

Doing that work well starts with doing excellent research—going beyond the world of mere opinions so easily available on the Internet and learning how to find, read, and use the kind of information on which true experts rely. Grand Valley's expert research librarians have developed "Information Literacy Core Competencies" (ILCCs) for college students, defining six main goals for college-level research.

According to the ILCCs, as a college-level researcher, you should learn to

- construct a question or problem statement,
- locate and gather information,
- evaluate sources,
- manage information,
- use information ethically, and
- communicate knowledge.

You will want to develop these abilities throughout your college career, but WRT 150 should give a strong basis in all these areas. In WRT 150 you will learn to construct research questions by developing a preliminary focus to help you manage the range of material that you might pursue. You will learn to create a plan for your search and identify the resources that will be available to help you (such as library guides, access to scholarly journals through online reference tools called "databases," and the research librarians themselves). You will learn to evaluate sources so that you use the most appropriate and effective materials rather than just the materials that pop up first in a web search. You will learn to manage information in ways that help you keep track of what you have found and lower the stress and anxiety of conducting complicated research. Of course, as we re-emphasize in many ways in this Guide, you will learn to use information ethically by giving other writers credit for what you have learned from them and for what they have written. By learning to cite sources correctly, you learn to avoid plagiarism, honor copyright, and participate expertly in academic discussions. Finally, we want you to communicate knowledge effectively by coming to understand the ways in which those academic discussions take place, and then by beginning to take your own place in those discussions.

We cannot overemphasize the importance of these information literacy competencies as part of an effective academic writing process. Information literacy does not always show up directly in grading criteria because it is essentially a process, not a product; yet information literacy will have a profound effect on the quality of your writing, and thus on your WRT 150 grades.

Furthermore, the benefits of information literacy go well beyond WRT 150. When you learn to include results from research into your writing effectively, you prepare yourself for success in later college work. Summarizing, paraphrasing, and quoting your sources effectively shows that you truly understand them. Citing and documenting your sources correctly proves not only that you understand your sources but also that you understand how academic writing works. Perhaps most importantly for first-year writers, working with sources in the right ways helps you to avoid charges of plagiarism. When we work with research sources, we have to take unusual care to make sure that readers know exactly what we are claiming as our own thinking and writing and exactly what came from someone else. We will resist discussing research, documentation, and plagiarism at great length here because all of that needs to be addressed far more extensively in your WRT 150 class. You must, however, be alert to the importance of using research material ethically in your WRT 150 experience.

Documenting Sources

We have referred above to "documentation" of sources, which may be a new term for you. Basically, "documentation" means giving readers a very precise way to know exactly where you got your language and information and when exactly you are using language or information from your sources. For example, you might have seen books that had "footnotes" at the bottom of the page, linked to small numbers inserted into the discussion. Those footnotes "document" the source of the information.

To make that reference work easier to do (in the long run!), academic writers have created several carefully defined "documentation styles," depending on the field or discipline in which they are writing. Most writers in the humanities use the documentation system of the Modern Language Association (MLA style), and this is the documentation style used most often in WRT 150 classes. Writers in the social sciences usually use the documentation system of the American Psychological Association (APA style), so some WRT 150 classes use, or at least permit, APA style. Both of these styles insert a brief reference to a source inside parentheses (often starting with an author's last name), and then add a list of sources at the end that you can find quickly by using the information in the parentheses. Most of the sample essays toward the end of this book use those documentation styles. If you have not worked with documentation very much, be sure to look at those examples so that you have a better idea of how they work.

You are likely to learn several documentation styles during your college career. We understand that this variety of documentation styles means that, for college students, documentation styles do not seem "easier" to use. Instead, they can seem confusing, trivial, picky, and even cruel. Please try to keep an open mind about them. By the time you are done with college, you will settle into some familiar styles for your work, and you will come to understand all the problems these documentation styles actually solve for you—problems that, right now, you probably could not even imagine. For now, you mainly need to remember that they are meant to be used precisely, and that their accurate use is your best method to avoid charges of plagiarism.

Avoiding Plagiarism

Certainly, you understand that you cannot have someone else do your writing for you or copy a paper and turn it in as your own. Most students also quickly understand the point of the Grand Valley policy forbidding submission of the same work in two different classes (including earlier high school classes)—at least unless you have permission from both instructors. Many first-year college students believe that as long as they avoid such extremely dishonest behavior, they cannot be accused of plagiarism; unfortunately, that belief is not correct.

Plagiarism is not simply a matter of dishonest intentions. Working with research sources requires writers to understand difficult aspects of plagiarism and make skilled, positive efforts to credit sources accurately and fully. Again, everyone knows that you cannot use the words of other writers without putting those words in quotation marks and giving the original writer credit. Many first-year students are surprised to find that, to avoid committing plagiarism, they also must do the following:

- Give credit to sources for their information and ideas as well as their words;
- Quote any exact phrases from the source, even if only a few words at a time, when they are included within your own sentences;

- Avoid using the same general sentence structure used by the source, except in exact and clearly marked quotations;
- Use your documentation style precisely to make perfectly clear when you are using material from a source and when you are presenting your own words and ideas.

In WRT 150, we expect students to learn more about documentation and avoiding plagiarism as the course goes on, so we may continue to work with your drafts even if they contain sections that might commit intentional or unintentional plagiarism. If you want more information about why we do that, read the statement by the national Council of Writing Program Administrators (CWPA) about best approaches to working with students on the concept of plagiarism, found online at http://www.wpacouncil.org/positions/WPAplagiarism.pdf.

Furthermore, we may not always see when you are using material from sources while we are working on your drafts. We rely on you to inform us of that. Nevertheless, by the end of the course, in your final portfolio, we will check closely for plagiarism and hold you entirely accountable for it according to the Grand Valley Student Code. Thus, you need to be sure that you understand how to document all your sources before the end of WRT 150. Be sure that you ask your teacher or consultants in the Writing Center about any instances of possible plagiarism in your work.

WRT 150 Student Resources

Computer Classrooms

While we do use other schedules and plans, WRT 150 classes generally meet twice a week, once in a traditional classroom and once in a computer classroom. Computer classrooms are sometimes used simply for writing and revising drafts, but your instructor may introduce a range of activities—brief in-class writing exercises, peer review sessions, and research assignments, for example—to help you gain expertise in a range of writing skills and strategies.

Any Grand Valley computer that you use in a computer classroom gives you the option to save items to a personal drive (the "N" drive), also known as your network account. You can access items saved to your network account from various campus locations, such as other campus computer labs and some campus living quarters, as well as from other Grand Valley campuses. You can also retrieve items on the N drive from an off-campus home computer. Seek assistance from Grand Valley's IT office (331-2101) for more information about file transfer.

The computer classrooms use recent versions of Microsoft Word, which is different from Microsoft Works, as the primary word-processing software. This means that Microsoft Works documents and some other documents do not open in a computer classroom unless you have saved them in a compatible format like rich-text format (.rtf), which you can do with nearly any word processing program. It also means that documents prepared in the computer classroom will not open on some other computers, especially older computers, unless you have saved them in rich-text format or another format used on that computer. Your teacher may be able to suggest other programs and methods for working on the same files both at home and in a computer classroom.

The Library and Online Library Resources

The goal of library-related instruction in WRT 150 is to help you become an information-literate lifelong learner who can use academic and professional research methods and sources. In order to reach this goal, you will learn how to develop and implement a research strategy, locate the resources necessary to meet your information needs, and evaluate the information that you find.

Many WRT 150 teachers work closely with Grand Valley librarians and bring librarians into class to help you learn how to use Grand Valley's libraries and online library resources. In addition, each class has a designated library liaison who will work with you on your research for WRT 150. Ask your teacher for the name of your library liaison, or feel free to ask library staff to help you find the right person. Many first-year college students do not understand that librarians in a college research library are eager and ready to offer substantial help to you, both in conducting your research and in learning how to become better researchers. Grand Valley's librarians are also faculty members who serve as part of our teaching staff. Ask for their help.

The Fred Meijer Center for Writing

Peer writing consultants work in all of the writing center locations as well as in WRT 098, WRT 150, and WRT 305 classes and in computer labs. Consultants do not simply check grammar and mechanics or guess what grade a paper may receive, but they do provide helpful feedback, offer advice, model writing strategies, and ask questions in order to help students improve as writers. Essentially, the role of a consultant is to provide a well-trained pair of eyes to help writers think more critically about their own writing, and to assist writers in devising a plan for revision.

Most WRT 150 teachers use computer classroom for consultations. In that setting, students have instant access to a consultant. Since consultants are trained across the board, they can discuss any issue that may arise while you are working through writing activities or drafting and revising your papers. For example, you might need a quick discussion about the purpose of topic sentences, a guided tour through the library's many online resources for research, or a more in-depth conference about a whole draft. Make a point to seek out your writing consultant often. When you establish a working relationship with your writing consultant, he or she will come to understand your unique writing strengths and challenges, and can offer advice that is useful for the specific purposes you have in mind for your writing projects.

Consultants also sometimes help to lead small-group discussions in WRT 150 classrooms. Small groups serve as a place to cultivate ideas, mold them into new shapes, and devise a plan for a paper. The consultant's role in these situations is to help the group stay on track, encourage everyone's involvement in the discussion, model or prompt the group to use effective feedback strategies, and offer another perspective on your writing.

Here are some tips for making your group discussions work:

- Come prepared with specific questions or areas of your writing for which you need feedback.
- Bring enough copies of your draft for each student and the consultant to have one. This allows your readers to follow along and write comments on the papers, which you might find helpful later

in your revision process.

- Solicit the advice of everyone in your group, not just the writing consultant. The more readers' ideas you have, the better idea you have about whether your writing is working.

In labs or small-group discussions, consultants are there as a resource to work through your individual writing needs. Get to know your classroom consultants early in the semester, and consider visiting them outside of class, too, when they are on duty in the writing center.

ood Writing in WRT 150

When we set out to choose portfolios to be published in this handbook, we don't try to anticipate which ones will serve as perfect models for future students. So what are we looking for when we begin the portfolio selection process? Our goal is to select writers who understand their papers' purposes, know what it is they are trying to accomplish in their work, and we look for authors who keep their audience in mind as they write. No matter what your assignment may be, the keys to good writing remain consistent—a solid sense of purpose, focus, and audience. But there are many portfolio essays that meet these requirements that are submitted for possible publication, so we try to choose pieces from writers that tackle diverse subject material. In showcasing work from previous WRT 150 students, we hope to open up classroom dialogue about the content as well as the writing. We have chosen six writers to showcase in this year's edition of the book and each has something special to offer.

Inspired by a Pablo Neruda poem, Marelguij Briones opens **Portfolio One** with "Brown and Agile Child," a memorable piece that chronicles the difficulties she experiences embracing her Mexican heritage. We see her wrestle with her cultural identity—from the language she speaks to the color of her skin. Marelguij's first-hand account realistically portrays how she comes to terms with who she is as a person. Strong narratives use sensory details to paint a word picture of a person, place, scene, object, or emotion. Such vivid and clear descriptions make stories come alive for readers. In her second essay, "The Skinny on Being Skinny," Briones writes poignantly about watching a loved one suffer from an eating disorder. Good research papers, like hers, start with a burning question: a question the writer is striving to find an answer to. For Marelguij, that question is: how did this happen to my sister? The essay demonstrates her ability to effectively utilize college-level academic research to develop her ideas and make greater sense of her sister's eating disorder. In a way, she is able to begin healing and discover how she can help in her sister's recovery. "How to Save a Home" covers another compelling topic—how to save the planet. Her essay has grand ambitions—to unite the United States in an attempt to better our world.

Instead of trying to tackle such a large topic, she decides to narrow it down to recycling and make the case for salvaging and reusing old materials. By doing so, she is able to progress from one point to another in a coherent, logical way. Through the art of persuasion, her essay convinces others why mandatory recycling is a viable option to save our home—Mother Earth. Marelguij's portfolio successfully demonstrates how students can incorporate their own experiences into their writing as a way to personally connect with the audience while creating deeper meaning for the reader.

Portfolio Two by Amanda Reed begins with a story about her childhood home, which in a way, comes to represent her family, and their future dreams. She colorfully captures the giddiness she felt as a little girl and all of the hopes that were tied into their 100-year-old farmhouse. Her mother and father have countless plans for the house, which never seem to come to fruition. The house, like the marriage, begins to show wear and tear with age. Through Amanda's candid reflection and emotional detail, we learn how the home she once loved becomes another unfulfilled promise from her father. As a whole, the essay has a meaningful pattern that maintains a consistent focus. In "Blinded by the Light," Reed critically explores the issue of light pollution and the harmful effects it has on humans and wildlife. As she writes, we see her take on the role of environmentalist and natural resources management major; allowing us to see how engaged she is with the subject matter. This engagement is carried on throughout her essay as she clearly articulates why excessive light is problematic with supporting evidence and detailed examples. There are no gaps of reasoning, unsupported assumptions or missing information that would cause a reader to stumble. In addition to presenting the problem, she also provides the audience with simple solutions to solve the issue. Doing so shows her deep commitment to the paper's topic, something instructors look for in quality portfolios. Amanda takes a fresh spin on "going green" in her closing piece "Modeling the Sustainability Movement." Many student writers, like Reed, find that the university setting often inspires great paper topics. Her essay discusses, through thorough description, how GVSU students can accelerate the sustainability movement via their education, practice and community involvement. All of her papers lead readers through orderly discussions that are explicit, clear, and purposeful. Amanda's careful topic selection and passion for her ideas is evident in each portfolio piece.

Joseph Early begins **Portfolio Three** with a heart-pounding tale of coming under siege while serving in the U.S. military in Iraq. His essay, "5.5lbs of Pressure," demonstrates a clear purpose as he recounts standing guard one night when the front gate of his base is suddenly attacked by mortar rounds and flying bullets. Joseph finds himself in a war zone that challenges his training as a soldier. The ensuing battle becomes a blur to Early, and while he is not physically wounded from the encounter, the mental wounds stay with him to this day. His dramatic recreation engages the interest of readers, allowing insight into a soldier's life and the realities of war. Joseph's second essay, "Social Media Influences on the 'Support the Troops' Campaign" investigates how U.S. military personnel have historically been treated by the American public after returning home from combat. During his first tour of duty he ponders how he will be accepted back into society. In his paper, he brings in a series of expert sources to more fully explore how the public has changed its opinion of the Iraq War, but acceptance of returning veterans has increased. He wonders why he was not treated like returning Vietnam veterans, when their war was so strongly criticized as well. His strong research skills enable him to locate the answers to those questions and demonstrate his ability to carefully synthesize and incorporate academic research. Information and quotations from sources are integrated skillfully into his sentences and paragraphs. Early ends his portfolio with an evaluative piece, "The Opera" which documents his reactions to a performance he attended at GVSU's Opera House. He does a great job critiquing the music, performance and costumes from a child's point of view. By viewing it through the eyes of who the performance was created for—children—he is able to appreciate the smiles of the kids leaving the opera. Joseph's portfolio highlights that good writing has a point or a goal to achieve. He carefully considers the relationship between content, purpose, and audience in each of his papers.

With her carefully crafted phrasing, an eye for detail, and graceful language, **Portfolio Four** by Leslie Kuhn offers readers a series of essays that are pleasurable to read. One of the biggest challenges when writing is creating a document that when read, feels to the reader as if it's all one seamless thread. She achieves this through the fluidity of her paragraph and sentence structure. "One Man's Trash" explores the trend of thrift shopping and the adventure of finding a bargain. In the essay, we learn how consumers are finally acknowledging the benefits of resale shopping, and how shopping at such stores is no longer considered taboo. Leslie makes a solid argument that thrift shopping can be a savvy, chic, and environmentally-friendly form of shopping. In "A Growing Industry and a Michigan Experience" Kuhn profiles a state vegetable that she believes does not receive the proper recognition it deserves—the asparagus. We learn that Michigan ranks third in the nation for their profitable asparagus production. Her richly descriptive passages highlight the humble family farmers who grow the crop, the zany festivals that pay homage to the vegetable, and the tender and flavorful taste of asparagus. Through substantially developed paragraphs, Leslie exposes how this slender green food is a major source of revenue not only for the Michigan economy as a whole, but also for local Michigan growers. Her creative approach to writing consistently engages the interests of a sophisticated college-level audience. In her final piece, "Grand Valley Weighs in on Poor Eating Habits and Lifestyle Choices," Kuhn takes on the national issue of obesity from a local perspective. By localizing it to campus, she is able to discover how a big-scale problem affects her local community. Through research she learns about GVSU students' poor lifestyle and eating choices and what university resources can be used to address it. Her references to outside sources are cited and documented according to the appropriate style guide so that readers can easily identify the sources that have been quoted or referenced. In addition, the focus of each of Leslie's portfolio papers is clearly emphasized and her overall writing is purposeful in nature.

Every life has a beginning and an end date, and in **Portfolio Five** Andrew Brown contemplates that little "dash" nestled between the dates. Using memories of his grandfather's life as a focal point, he questions what his dash will mean. The meaning of his own life becomes clear as he reflects on memories of his dying grandfather. As a writer, Brown makes the audience part of his journey. He reveals personal emotions and insights that help readers better understand the significance of his story. Andrew ultimately realizes we only have so much time, and we have to make the best of what we have with the people who mean the most—friends and family. In "Does Your Mother See Those Grades?" he confronts student-athletes'

Personal Feelings, Experiences Ect.

gradesin college and places the blame on the intercollegiate athletic system and universities. He asks, "How can we expect these kids to do well when they're set up to fail?" Andrew writes with fire and authority. He has a definite voice and doesn't hold back his opinions. While he uses quality academic sources, he still maintains his own unique voice. Something WRT 150 teachers encourage their students to do. In his final essay, "To Some a Game, to Others Something More," Brown profiles Elliot Uzelac, coach of the St. Joseph Bears. He produces an intriguing and well-focused portrait of Coach U's coaching style and relationship with the community. Readers can easily visualize the town's pride in the football program as we drive through St. Joe with Andrew and see maize and blue signs that say "Bear Country" decorating just about every yard. His personal interview reveals the recipe for a winning team—engaged kids, active parents, and an invested community. First-year college writers often feel intimidated by the concept of voice. In writing, voice is the way your writing "sounds" on the page. It has to do with the way you write, the tone you take, the words you choose and the pattern of your sentences, and the way these things fit into your paper overall. Papers, like Andrew's, illustrate how students can produce portfolios with effective style and strong voice.

Megan Kuckuk's works in **Portfolio Six** each begin with an engaging introduction that sets the tone for the rest of the paper. Titles and opening sections inform readers appropriately of the topic, purpose, and focus of the paper and motivates them to read further. In her first essay, Megan invites us into the pool with her as she attempts to gain confidence in her swimming abilities. Her narrative paints a vivid portrait of her high school swimming career and all of its ups and downs. With each turn of the page, the audience gets an emotional temperature for her character and what she is going through. Her four years of growing pains to become a better swimmer unfold on the paper as Kuckuk intimately reflects on what it took for her to get there. We root for her from the stands as she makes her way to the senior finish line as the leader she always wanted to be. Megan follows with "White Head Phones and the Disconnect" which chronicles the social and physical damage that iPods and MP3 players are having on this generation. She persuasively argues that personal listening devices have a negative impact on society because they decrease social interaction, further disconnect people, and damage hearing. She foresees a society becoming strangled by these little white wires. Her essay is extremely persuasive in that she cites specific examples and facts to fully support her points. Kuckuk formally introduces her sources and their level of expertise to further back up her claims. Megan's paragraphs are purposefully organized and substantially developed with supporting evidence, examples, and reasoning. "Take Nothing but Photographs, Leave Nothing but Foot Prints" focuses on urban explorers, a subculture made up of people who choose not to follow the mainstream opinion of what is beautiful and what is off limits. According to Megan, urban explorers find beauty in crumbling man-made structures and abandoned places containing rich history. Her paper captures this community's insatiable curiosity and why they desire creativity and adventure. She makes you want to do some urban exploring of your own. Kuckuk's portfolio is filled with interesting topics that demonstrate her ability to perform college-level writing, research, and thinking.

We invite WRT 150 instructors and students to read and discuss these six portfolios as a way to generalize about what characterizes good writing in the first-year writing program at Grand Valley State University. As you read, notice the similarities and differences from portfolio to portfolio— the kinds of writing included, the number and types of sources cited, the length of the papers, and so on. Keep in mind that hundreds of other students wrote quality portfolios last fall and winter, and although they were probably as diverse in subject material as the essays exemplified here, all the writers understood the keys to good writing—composing with a solid sense of purpose, focus, and audience.

Marelguij Briones
WRT 150

Brown and Agile Child

I was extraordinarily rich when I was young. Not rich in monetary wealth, but rich with culture and heritage. Each and every one of my senses was augmented by the sensory stimulators abundant in my home. My house was perpetually brimming with succulent, exotic smells: the sharp bite of pasilla and poblano peppers sizzling over a pan on my mother's stove, the sugary sweetness of warm Mexican bread, the familiar scent of pillowy soft tortillas wafting across the kitchen floor. I can still feel the refreshing coolness of the cold mosaic tiles beneath my feet, soothing my calloused and sun burnt skin. The walls resonated with swaying music, the pulsating rhythms of salsa and samba somehow harmonizing perfectly with the velvety tones of bossa nova. I adored listening to my family converse— their fast-paced Spanish murmurs, flowing as smooth and rich as honey, whispering in the background. In the summer months my backyard would be swollen with the dizzying asphyxiation of sunlight-blotted calla lilies, illuminated by the white-hot rays of sun, the moist, black soil heaving the tang of earth into the air. The hammock pressed diamonds into my back as I rocked in the breeze, and I enjoyed the pleasurable taste of a mushy guava brought back from a trip to Mexico while my bed of rope serenely lulled me to sleep.

I recall these memories with a great deal of fondness. I look back at my childhood and am indubitably aware of how fortunate I was to have been exposed to a culture so abounding in customs and tradition. However, having been raised in an area predominantly populated by whites, it was sometimes difficult for me to embrace my culture. Both my parents are Mexican; my father was born in Mexico and immigrated to the United States with his family at eight years old, my mother lived in Mexico City until the day she married my father, upon which she then moved to the small town of Pacoima, California to be with him. Though I was born in California, my parents feared the growing crime rate and, shortly after I was born, deemed it the appropriate time for a change of scenery. They uprooted themselves from the increasing urbanization in the city my father had called home for forty years and moved clear across the country to the

Marelguij wrote her portfolio in the class of Professor Arlene Hecksel.

Midwest, where I spent my childhood growing up in suburban Michigan. The neighborhood we lived in was as safe as any parents' most desirable dream. It provided us with a sense of security in our home, friendly neighbors, plenty of parks and playgrounds for the many children residing in the subdivision, and numerous nearby elementary schools. One of these was a private Catholic school located close to our home that I attended from first grade until the end of junior high. During the eight years I attended St. Gerard School, the only other minorities in my grade apart from me was an African-American student and one Indian-American student. I was the only Mexican.

As it would be expected, being the only one of my kind, so to speak, distinguished me from others. Based on appearances alone there were many differences that caused me to stand out. My skin coloring, a burnt caramel brown, may as well have been on an entirely different color palette in comparison to the one of my friends. I never possessed the fair, freckly flush of the coveted Anglo-Saxon complexion; instead, I all but blended into the shadows with my uneven, blackened tone. More often than not I was teased for my thick smearing of eyebrows, the less-than-feminine black fuzz stretching along my jaw line and above my upper lip, the warped and distorted pronunciation and spelling of my name, and my undeniably stunted growth. Out of the sixty or so classmates in my grade I was the smallest one. By the time I was in the fourth grade the majority of my peers looked down on me by a foot at the very least. Not only did my looks and height disadvantage set me apart from the rest of my uniform-clad classmates, but the fact that I also spoke an entirely different language added to that effect.

My mother wanted her children to fit into American culture and the typically accepted norms associated with it; she may not have vocally advocated for assimilation but neither did she ever discourage my brother and me away from it. Yet my mother's most profound fear was that her children would not be able to communicate in the language of her ancestors, that we would reject the Spanish tongue and refuse to learn to speak it. So she determinedly drilled the words and the phonetics and the grammar into me until I could speak, read, and write Spanish fluently. Being bilingual in this day and age is a blessing with countless advantages. Nonetheless, this foreign dialect served as a constant reminder of the cultural barrier preventing me from being what I considered to be a true American. With this mindset

I brought the feeling of humiliation upon myself, and with that a sense of shame, my gaze darkening and my brows narrowing whenever my parents spoke to me in Spanish in the terrible exposure of any public place. I came to resent the language my family spoke; "speak English," I would demand desperately. All of these differences added to the difficulty I experienced growing up in coming to terms with my nationality.

I wish I could recount a touching story of an impacting experience I had that suddenly caused me to accept my ethnic background all at once, perhaps an epiphany of some sort that made me proud to be Mexican. However that was not the case. I would continue to struggle through my misguided shame as I got older. I would still be teased by classmates and I would still experience moments of weakness where I would shrink away from my peers' curious questions about my culture. Even to this day I sometimes feel uncomfortable with some aspects of my family's customs. Nevertheless, I have reached a point in my life where I have come to terms with who I am. It may not have come easily but I now take pride in my heritage and am proud of how I was raised. I have realized I do not want to live my life trying to please others or diminishing myself so as to not call attention to the things that make me different. The cultural traditions my parents incorporated into my life growing up helped mold me into the person I am today. The smells and tastes I was accustomed to as a child influenced my love of food and trying new things. I play the piano in a rhythmically Latin form because of the type of music that was played in my home. I possess a unique perspective in relation to words and how they function in a sentence due to the knowledge I have gained by being able to communicate in two languages. My culture is very beautiful and exceptionally complex and it adds a deeper essence to my life that I would not possess without it.

Though there was never an epiphany that instantly changed my viewpoint on my heritage, I did experience a moment of realization that aided me in my journey. Many years ago my father gave me a gift. This gift was a book of compiled poems by the famous Chilean poet and politician Pablo Neruda. One of these poems has remained imprinted in my mind since the day I first read it:

Brown and agile child, the sun which forms the fruit and twists the seaweed has made your happy body and your luminous eyes and given your mouth the smile of water. A black and anguished sun is entangled in the twigs of your black mane. You play in the sun as in a tidal river and it leaves two dark pools in your eyes. You are the delirious youth of bee, the drunkedness of the wave, the power of the heat. (Neruda)

I am that child. I am that brown and agile child, the embodiment of a culture that radiates heat and passion. This poem describes the view I have of my heritage that has developed over the years. I have come to the realization that my skin color does not isolate me, rather it connects me to other ways of life and brings people together as the warmth of the sun brings them closer to one another in the enjoyment of each other's company. Whenever I fail to feel pride in my people and their traditions, I simply remember this passage and think about what it means to me. I have come a long way since being that small brown child with the black and anguished sun entangled in her black mane, ashamed of her family's traditions and the customs she grew up with. I am no longer that child, but a brown and agile child with a happy body and luminous eyes that shine with the mysteries and customs of her culture. I am "the delirious youth of bee, the drunkedness of the wave, the power of the heat."

Marelguij Briones
Writing 150

The Skinny on Being Skinny: The Reality of Eating Disorders and the
Hope in Overcoming Them

Nine months. This is the amount of time it takes a cell to develop into a living being. Nine months is how long a typical school year usually lasts. Nine months is the period of time it takes most infants to utter their first word or even take their first step. This is also how long it took my sister to admit she was being eaten away by anorexia nervosa. It took nine months for my sister to finally realize she could count every chest bone and rib stretching through the thin layer of skin on her upper body. It took nine months for her to admit that losing fistfuls of hair every time she ran her fingers through it was not normal. It took nine months for my sister to decide she could no longer stand to weigh herself every time she ate and refuse to eat for the remainder of the day if she weighed .2 of a pound more than usual. It took nine months for her to become conscious of the fact that, as an eighteen-year-old, she was now the same size she was when she was twelve. It took nine months for my sister to ask for help, and it took me nine months to finally understand that I was the one who needed to help her.

The two main types of eating disorders are anorexia nervosa and bulimia nervosa. Anorexia nervosa is characterized by emaciation, a relentless pursuit of thinness and unwillingness to maintain a normal or healthy weight, a distortion of body image and intense fear of gaining weight, a lack of menstruation among girls and women, and extremely disturbed eating behavior. Some people with anorexia lose weight by dieting and exercising excessively; others lose weight by self-induced vomiting, or misusing laxatives, diuretics or enemas. Eating, food, and weight control become obsessions. A person with anorexia typically weighs herself repeatedly, portions food carefully, and eats only small quantities of only certain foods. Bulimia nervosa is characterized by recurrent and frequent episodes of eating unusually large amounts of food, and feeling a lack of control over the eating. This binge-eating is followed by a type of behavior that compensates for the binge, such as purging, fasting or excessive exercise. Similar to those struggling with anorexia, people with bulimia often fear gaining weight, want desperately to lose weight or are intensely unhappy with their body size and shape ("Eating Disorders"). Both are extremely prevalent in the United States, though Medical News Today states, "while anorexia is much discussed in the media, there are twice as many people with bulimia" (qtd. in "Anorexia and Bulimia"). Regardless, bulimia and anorexia together form the third most common illness among adolescent females (Cornell). A third category is Eating Disorders Not Otherwise Specified (EDNOS), which includes several variations of eating disorders. Most of these disorders are similar to anorexia or bulimia but with slightly different characteristics. Binge-eating disorder, which has received increasing research and media attention in recent years, is one type of EDNOS ("Eating Disorders").

My sister suffers from anorexia nervosa. She displayed the three most prevalent signs of the disorder according to Help Guide, a trusted mental and emotional health resource: the refusal to maintain a healthy body weight, an intense fear of gaining weight, and a distorted body image ("Anorexia Nervosa"). My sister is four feet, eleven inches tall and currently weighs ninety-five pounds. She is tiny. At the height of her disorder, her lowest weight was eighty-four pounds, and even then she felt as though she could stand to be even thinner. Along with these psychological symptoms, she showed signs of many of the physical indications of anorexia as well. The discontinuation of her menstrual cycle, hair loss, weakness and fatigue, bloating, moodiness and depression, dry and cold skin, a growth of fine hair over her body and face...my sister had it all. We as a society clearly have a relatively organized structure set up to help us categorize the different types of eating disorders into groups based on the symptoms. However, what I have difficulty understanding is where these disorders come from in the first place. I look at how far my sister has come and think back to all the pain she went through and cannot help wondering – why did it happen to her?

Counselors at Remuda Ranch and Sierra Tucson (in-patient treatment centers) often find that relatives of patients with eating disorders struggle with depression, manic-depressive disorders, alcoholism, or eating disorders themselves which suggests a possible genetic predisposition. Other psychiatrists follow the book and call it a disease (Cornell). In any case, one of the leading causes of eating disorders is a personality with a tendency toward perfectionist and controlling qualities. Dr. Craig Johnson, in his article "The Many Causes of Eating Disorders," reveals that eating disorder patients can be perfectionists with very high achievement expectations. For these individuals, losing weight through self-starvation can be seen as the first step to improving themselves. In addition, many who suffer from eating disorders experience a tremendous fear of losing control or not being in control. For a significant number of these individuals, anorexia is a misguided, but understandable, attempt at remaining in control of their lives. Most individuals who develop eating disorders do not usually perceive their behaviors as self-harmful. Actually, most patients feel that they began the behaviors to try to fix other problems. The most common reason therapists hear from people about why they began self-starvation, bingeing or purging is that at some point they felt terribly out of control – whether because of something they were feeling inside themselves or something that was happening to them from their outside environment (Johnson).

My sister exhibits all the personality traits listed above. She is a perfectionist, expecting nothing but the absolute best from herself. My sister has always valued taking pride in herself with excellent grades, a charismatic personality, and being the star athlete in sports. With this, of course, comes her unfailing propensity to place an enormous amount of importance on appearance. My sister has the misguided inclination to look down on people she believes do not put enough effort into maintaining an outward impression of beauty in the public eye. She is also controlling, always taking charge and immediately appointing herself as the leader in every situation. She despises feeling helpless. It seems my sister experienced a certain thrill through the act of restricting her caloric intake. Among the struggles and preoccupations she faced at school and at work, the extent to which she could control how much food she consumed was almost like a dangerous, wild adventure. Waking up each morning and seeing her weight plummet day by day was ecstasy for her, as was not knowing just how far she could push herself until she had to stop.

Another personality trait commonly observed in people with eating disorders is the tendency to resist change. Many patients with eating disorders have difficulty with change. Anorexics, in particular, typically prefer things to be predictable, orderly, and familiar. Consequently, transitions such as the onset of puberty, entering high school or college, or major illness or death of someone close to them can overwhelm these individuals and cause them to feel a loss of control. In many girls with eating disorders, the lowering of body weight and body fat levels from self-starvation can arrest the menstrual cycle and delay other body changes that come with puberty. Girls who lose their period essentially return to a more childlike state, both physically and psychologically. They neither feel nor look like adolescent or young adult women and can therefore postpone making the transition to adolescence or young adulthood (Johnson).

This description fits my sister perfectly. My sister hates change. She hates it. I often tell her she is the female version of Peter Pan. For some reason my sister had some difficulty leaving behind childhood, she faced it with tremendous resistance. She never had any problems maturing. In fact, she was always quite mature even at a very young age; it was just the transition into adolescence that proved to be challenging. Could she have had things her way, she would have kept everything in her life exactly the same. It was as if that one carefree point in her life, that period during childhood in which she was the happiest, continued to dictate her way of living even after those years were long gone. The time for my sister to go off to college was approaching and I sometimes wonder whether that might have triggered a defense mechanism in her subconscious, postponing that transition.

My sister continues to rage her battle against anorexia nervosa…the difference now, however, is that she is winning. She has spoken with a psychologist who specializes in eating disorders and regularly attends nutrition counseling. She has found the undeniable comfort of a support group in many different places: in an on-campus Christian ministry that has taught her the value of internal beauty, in our family who gives her strength through love and prayer, in her closest friends who anchor her if ever a moment of weakness threatens to strike and…in me. For I have taken this journey with her. I have lived her lowest moments and I have witnessed her darkest days through her eyes. I have experienced that same desperation and desolateness she felt, the wretched frustration that came with her inability to overpower her illness. With her I cried for her situation, at the sheer incomprehension of its hold on her, on us, and the despondency of its seemingly interminable reign. I cried also at the joy of return, the return of life into her body, her incessantly cold limbs now revived with color and warmth. I admit I took her beauty for granted before her encounter with anorexia, not in terms of superficiality but more in regard to the beauty of loving herself; I am reminded of the endeavor that went into making her the strong, resilient young woman she is today each and every time I look at her. It has been nine months now since she first asked for help, and nine months since I realized I was the one who was to help her. The only distinction now is that she has arrived at the realization that she must also be the one to help herself.

Works Cited

"Anorexia and Bulimia." *Medical News Today*. MediLexicon International Ltd., 5 Sept. 2004. Web. 3 Mar. 2011.

"Anorexia Nervosa: Signs, Symptoms, Causes, and Treatment." *Help Guide. A Trusted Non-Profit Resource* (2001): n. pag. Web. 3 Mar. 2011.

Cornell, Laurel L. "Where Do Eating Disorders Come From?" *Focus on the Family* (1999): n. pag. Web. 3 Mar. 2011.

"Eating Disorders." *National Institute of Mental Health*. 24 Aug. 2010. Web. 3 Mar. 2011.

Johnson, Craig. "The Many Causes of Eating Disorders." *Healthy Place: America's Mental Health Channel*. 5 Dec. 2008. Web. 3 Mar. 2011.

Marelguij Briones
Writing 150

How to Save a Home

Nothing is more breathtaking than feeling the warmth of the sun's rays caressing your face through leaves of deep green on a cool spring afternoon. The regality of the trees standing proudly so tall and so wise invokes such a sense of heartfelt feeling within me; it makes me almost want to cry, especially when this image of splendor is observed in comparison with an entirely different image. This second image is one of despair, a picture perfect paradigm of the damage we as human beings have caused. This illustration is a depiction of gray skies where the skyscrapers and acid rain prevent the sunlight from reaching the earth. It exposes naked forests containing nothing but slashed trunks of the grand trees they once held, wounds representing the pathetic remnant of what was once powerful and commanding. It is commonly believed that pollution and the lack of consideration for the environment have pushed the earth past its ability to reveal the majestic beauty it once possessed. While this may be true in some aspects of the world, many of the consequences can still be reversed. This particular subject raises a strong passion within me because, for me, there is nothing worse than looking around at what used to be so awe-inspiring and seeing it reduced to such a sorry, regret-inducing state. What prompted us as mere tenants of this earth to abandon all morality and exchange it instead for a small-scale dose of industrialization and modernization? I understand the issues people have against this statement, I am sure the majority of the world's population would stand firmly in the belief that a minor sacrifice of the earth's overall cleanliness is a price worth paying to achieve the ideal mechanized world. However, when we truly stop and take the time to delve deeper into the potential consequences, both those we are already experiencing and the ones sure to come, it is astoundingly clear that the damage to the earth is far greater than the benefits we may be receiving. Fortunately, there are steps we can take to begin saving our beautiful home.

The problem with our society is that there is not enough emphasis being placed on recycling and the reduction of disposing what could be recycled in landfills. According to "Eco Green Living and All Recycling Facts," a website designed specifically with the intention of exposing the shocking facts and statistics of recycling, entire forests are being cut at the astounding rate of one hundred acres per minute. It takes a plant a minimum of fifteen to twenty years to grow into a tree, but only ten minutes to be cut; this one tree is used to yield approximately 700 paper grocery bags, which are consumed in less than one hour by one supermarket. These bags, which are used for a couple of minutes at most to transport a few groceries to the car and to the home, are then thrown away to lay useless in a dump for eternity. If this is what occurs solely in one solitary hour, in one supermarket, the destruction of just one tree, can we even truly imagine the extent of this reality when it comes to a day, or an entire week, or numerous years? I really do not think we understand the magnitude of this situation. What I do understand, however, is that this is completely unacceptable. Therefore, being aware of this information and deliberately choosing not to be proactive about it is, in my opinion, incredibly irresponsible. This same website states that for every ton of paper that is recycled, seventeen trees, 60,000 gallons of water, 225 kilowatt hours, and 3.3 cubic yards of landfill space are saved ("Eco Green"). The United States remains the world's leading "throwaway society," according to the article "The Economics of Recycling" written by Mary H. Cooper, a researcher for CQ Press. She points out that every week more than 500,000 trees are used to produce two-thirds of newspapers that are never recycled [in the United States]. Americans also throw away enough office and writing paper annually to build a wall twelve feet high from Los Angeles to New York City, and throw away enough glass bottles and jars to fill two 1,350-feet towers every two weeks (Cooper). The degree to which our country is willing to extend a blind eye to the detrimental effects being caused by our ignorance is grotesque and must be put to an end.

One of the consequences that is affecting our nation is a higher fuel price. The article "Increasing Sustainability: A Study of Recycled Materials" states that producing more aluminum, textiles, plastic, paper, and other brand new materials from scratch will consume far more energy than salvaging and reusing old materials. The more brand new products that must be created, the more energy used and the less fuel available, which results in higher fuel prices. Nonetheless, a higher fuel price is not the sole negative consequence affecting the country. Along with higher fuel prices, contaminated drinking water and an increase in the number of landfills are also consequences of not recycling ("Increasing Sustainability"). These are all things that can be prevented by recycling if we catch them in time.

One possible option for fixing this problem is establishing mandatory recycling. This is not a new idea; the pros and cons of instituting national laws forcing citizens to recycle have been conferred about for quite some time. A large part of the resistance this idea has been met with stems from how much it would cost the country. In relation to the cost of mandatory recycling, we can examine those places that have already put such laws or similar laws into place. For example, an article that appeared in Business Today, "Benefits of Recycling Worth Costs," outlines the mandatory recycling law passed in Wisconsin in 1990 and its legislature, which currently funds the state's recycling programs. Mike Ivey with The Capital Times writes, "The [recycling] fund has helped many communities get their recycling programs off the ground," a statement that contributes to the general argument that if the government were to provide that extra push, people would become accustomed to the idea and build upon it.

An excellent example of this can be seen in Wisconsin. When there was talk of reducing the recycling funding, Representative Spencer Black [agreed] it would be a mistake to trim too much state support for recycling programs. While Black admits that recycling has proven more costly than many advocates had hoped, he says there are other benefits that often are not considered: 2,000 new jobs in Wisconsin, a fifty percent reduction in waste going into landfills, and a savings of seventy million dollars in resources (Ivey 1C). This statement is a perfect example of the benefits of recycling outweighing the costs. It may be true that, if a law should be passed making recycling mandatory, it would cost more money than simply disposing of anything and everything in a landfill, yet there are so many more benefits to recycling. Wisconsin alone is not the only example of a success story in the establishment of recycling programs. Former EPA Assistant Administrator J. Winston Porter, now president of the Waste Policy Center, a research and consulting firm in Leesburg, [Virginia], states, "When I announced the 25 percent goal, only about 12 percent of the nation's garbage was recycled," he says. "The recycling rate grew pretty rapidly, and our goal was reached in 1995" (qtd. in Cooper). Many states have already begun setting goals; all that needs to be done now is follow through and come up with methods to achieve them.

Mandatory recycling is not a far-fetched idea. Yes, it will take added effort and yes, it will cost money. However, with a little endeavor it is possible to unite the United States in a nationwide aspiration to better our world. We have the resources, we have the funds, the only thing missing is the dedication and perseverance to actually do it. We are running out of time to fix the problem before it becomes too late and it is absolutely crucial we take action. If we continue in the direction we are going at right now, negative consequences will not be far to follow.

The world we live in is a truly exceptional place, we should take pride in it and take it upon ourselves to be responsible and protect it. It is essential that we take into account the potential consequences the future could bring and how it would affect the generations to follow. An easy way to do this is by establishing a law making recycling mandatory. We have already seen the success it has brought in Wisconsin and Virginia and I stand firmly in the belief that it would bring the same level of accomplishment to Michigan and other U.S. states if put into effect. The next time you find yourself enjoying the wonders of nature, take a moment to ask yourself if this moment would be as pleasurable if you were simultaneously being engulfed in a tsunami of litter and trash.

Works Cited

Burnett, Royce, Mark Friedman, Vaidyanathan Jayaraman, and Jonathan West. "Increasing Sustainability: A Study of Recycled Materials." *The International Journal of Environmental, Cultural, Economic, and Social Sustainability* 3.4 (2008): 1-14. Print.

Cooper, Mary H. "The Economics of Recycling – Is It Worth the Effort?" *The CQ Researcher* 8.12 (2011): n. pag. Web. 1 Feb. 2011.

"Eco Green Living & All Recycling Facts – Every Bit Counts." *All-recycling-facts.* 2009. Web. 18 Jan. 2011.

Ivey, Mike. "Benefits of Recycling Worth Costs." *Madison Capital Times.* 1997: 1C. Print.

Amanda Reed
Writing 150

The House with No Walls

I wrap my hands around the handle of the sledge hammer and start to swing. The first hit bounces off the wall without leaving much of a dent, so I choke up on the handle a little bit, watching my older brother to make sure I'm doing it right. I have to twist my whole body around to get the five-pound hammer through the lath and caked plaster. This project was my mom's idea, but it was my idea of fun. As we hammer away and pry off the debris, we expose hundred-year-old, rough-hewn studs, dark like chocolate, and nails like I've never seen before. They look more like wedges of metal, with a tiny cap on the end, and they're flat instead of round like other nails. They're cool, so I shove a few in my pocket for show-and-tell. Plaster chunks and dust cake the floor and cloud the air, making the air scratchy when I breathe. Thin, splintered pieces of wood lath are strewn everywhere. I'm covered in sweat, and it makes my clothes stick to me like they're too tight. Every muscle aches, but the sense of destruction is exhilarating. My heart is pumping away inside, and if it weren't for my dinky little muscles, I could have gone on all day long. By the time we finished for the day, we'd succeeded in making the biggest mess I'd ever seen and denuded every wall on the second floor of our house. That was by far my favorite part of building our house; smashing the old walls to bits was great fun. No other six-year-old had ever had so much fun.

Looking back on my childhood, that day is one of the few days that I can remember clearly. The work had finally begun on the house, and as we sat to eat subs for a late lunch, we admired our triumph of destruction. That exhilarating demolition signified the beginning of turning our dream home into a reality. I can still feel the giddiness that I felt as a little girl, and all the hope that was tied up into that house. That kind of hope would be short-lived, and I wish more than anything that I could have bottled it up and kept it safe. That day, my brother and I could barely wait to see our dad's reaction when he got home and saw how much we had accomplished while he was at work. As I looked around at the bare walls and mess, I saw the rooms that my dad had promised beginning to take shape.

Amanda wrote her portfolio in the class of Professor Julie White.

Those dreams had begun a year earlier, when my parents bought a dilapidated hundred-year-old farm house. It was listed as a handy-man special, though in reality the house should have been condemned. It was home to me for ten years, all of my childhood as far as I could remember. Our tree house was in the back yard, and our dog was buried beneath the bushes on the side of the house. When we first bought our home, the future was bright. The rickety old house seemed more like a palace to my naive eyes. The rutted gravel driveway led up to a two-story house that was all our own, no more trailer park, no more living with Grandma. I'd have my own room, and a huge backyard to play in. There were huge trees in the front yard, and a wide open field all around it, and beautiful lilac bushes that lined the drive. Later in the year we'd find a patch of blackberries that became a repeating joy every summer after; my fingers were annually stained blackberry-purple as my mother begged us to leave a few behind for her to make pies. It was going to be our dream home.

Soon after we moved in Dad brought home a large paper tube, and with a ridiculously cheesy grin, set it on the table for Mom to open. She uncapped it and rolled out the large papers inside, unceremoniously using coasters to hold the corners. Dad had used a huge printer at work to print up real blueprints for the house. I was so excited it felt like I'd jump right out of my skin as Dad pointed out the highlights.

"This is the wrap-around porch, and the gazebo," he said, pointing to a picture of the front of the house, "and this is what the inside will look like." He shifted the pages so we could see the next two, and I tried to figure out which way the plans were facing in relation to where I sat at the table and what it would look like inside.

Our parents talked over the plans: an addition on the back of the house, two more bedrooms, two more bathrooms, a laundry room; while my brother and I thought over more important things. My room would have a garden painted on the wall, and flowers on the carpet, and I wouldn't have to share a bunk bed with my older brother, whose primary occupation in life was to torture me. His room would be football themed, with green turf carpeting, and I wouldn't be allowed in it, he informed. I sat at our rickety old kitchen table, imagining what it would look like without the puke-green carpet and cheesy-yellow linoleum.

"When will it be done?" I beamed up at my dad, the purveyor of all these dreams.

"Well, as long as I have some help, we should be able to pour the foundation for the addition this spring, then do the roof and siding by fall." At his reply, Mom glowed. I had never seen her so happy.

The spring came and went with no foundation, and snow fell without any work on the roof or siding. So my mother began to strip the inside walls to the studs, officially beginning the project, and hoping it would induce my father to begin his share of the work. When he came home from work to see his children beaming and the walls laid bare, he was not as happy as my brother and I had expected him to be. He certainly wasn't as motivated as my mom had hoped. So Mom stapled black plastic on the exterior walls, and hung blankets for doors. The bathroom was the only room in the house that had all four walls covered with plastic. I could reach through the studs next to my bed, and pull clothes off the rack in the closet, and there was a short-cut between every room if you could fit between the studs. There was also a shortcut through the thin plywood stairs, which my foot slipped into on occasion when I missed the middle support.

Several years went by, with a little work done each year, before the foundation was laid for the addition, and not long after the shell was completed, the money ran out. Dad blamed their finances and terrible credit; Mom blamed his affinity for spending every penny he earned; and my brother and I stayed in our tree house and avoided the fighting as much as we could. The fields surrounding the house and the small grove of trees behind it welcomed us, and became more of a home than the actual house. The outside of the house was covered with silver-coated foam, which had deep red lettering to show off its brand name. Before the siding was put on the house, the lettering had faded away, the silver had bleached off, and my parents had divorced. The house was sold. All our dreams unfinished.

My dad was like the house, full of so many promises, so much left unfinished. He's always starting, never finishing. When I was young, I would listen to him talk about a business plan, and think he was an amazingly intelligent man, that these plans would succeed and fix all our problems. I wanted to be just like him: a dreamer. When the company he worked for went out of business, he used our savings to buy up a chunk of their equipment to start his own tool and die company, and built a pole barn as big as our house for it. He designed a logo with a steep mountain peak, and named the company "Apex", and never used any of the equipment even once. He later started a publishing company, photography business, and even joined a get-rich-quick pyramid scheme. He never actually published a book, and only took a handful of pictures before deciding it wasn't for him. But his business plans and house plans weren't the only things he didn't follow through on. So many times he promised to take me hunting. I've never been. Fishing; once. Hiking; once.

We spent so many hours talking about the wonderful trips we would take. For my high school graduation, we'd take one massive hiking trip in the Appalachian Mountains. The map of the Appalachian Trail, along with several maps for smaller hiking trips we'd take leading up to it, were the only décor on the walls of our apartment. We bought and read guide books, and I got a new external frame backpack and mummy-style down sleeping bag. Every spring, these promises were made anew, and every fall held the same apologies and excuses. When my senior year finally came, his plans had changed. His new girlfriend didn't like hiking, and didn't appreciate him spending time with his daughter. That was when I finally learned my lesson, and I stopped listening. I learned that dreams were only open invitations to pain and disappointment, and I made a conscious decision to slam the door and bolt it shut.

It wasn't until I was married and had kids of my own that I saw our house again, the beginning to all that pain and disappointment. It was on the market, and only an hour away, so I convinced my husband to drive down and see it one last time. It was finished, with a deck instead of a wrap-around, and no gazebo. It looked nothing like the plans that we had drawn up. They had painted our pole-barn a cliché shade of red and sold off almost all the property. Instead of the wide-open fields that had once welcomed me, there were typical ranch homes clustered close together in their manicured lawns. I ran down the path behind the barn, running before my husband could see the tears beginning to fall, and hoping for the same comfort that I had once found on this same path. I remembered the slope that had once been there, the exact number of steps to where the creek had run into a muck-bottomed pond. The only thing left was a small grove of familiar trees. Some of them had been cut down, but the ones that were left I knew well, and ran my hands over their bark to say goodbye. Our tree house and blackberries were gone. As I walked back up the driveway to the car, I cried for the house that never was, home-sick for a home that never would be. But it really wasn't the house I was looking for; I didn't want to buy it and try to regain what was lost. As I had walked the land and looked at the house, I was looking for memories that I had long lost. I was looking for the girl that used to live there, the girl that knew how to dream.

Amanda Reed
Writing 150

Blinded by the Light

Before Edison experimented with filaments under glass, the night was illuminated by the moon and by the glow of starlight. Any activities past dark were carried out by candlelight or lantern, or not at all. Over more than a hundred and thirty years, electric lights slowly crept into the world, forever changing the nightscape ("Edison's"). Lights cover store fronts and parking lots, and street lamps blaze along highways, main streets, and side streets indiscriminately. The orange glow over our cities and suburbs blots out all but the brightest stars. While some of these lights extend our productive and social day and illuminate our streets for safety, when they become inefficient, overly bright, or glaring, they cause what is known as light pollution (International Dark, Practical Guide 1, 2). According to Ron Chepesiuk, an investigative journalist and professor at UCLA, light pollution is being recognized by environmentalists, naturalists, and medical researchers as "one of the fastest growing, most pervasive forms of environmental pollution." It's difficult to consider something as simple as excess light as a problematic pollutant, but it causes serious concerns that have nothing to do with astronomy. Exposure to excessive light has serious effects on wildlife and human health, but light pollution, despite its pervasion, has simple solutions, including the use of shielded light-fixture designs and reduction of unnecessary outdoor lighting.

One of the significant problems with light pollution is light trespass, defined by the International Dark-Sky Association as "light falling where it is not intended, wanted, or needed." The sea turtle is one example of a charismatic endangered species that is affected by this kind of light pollution. In his article, "Missing the Dark", Ron Chepesiuk states that egg-laying females prefer darkened beaches to nest, and when hatchlings emerge, they are drawn toward the moonlight reflecting off the ocean and away from the dark backdrop of the beach. When development near the shore creates an artificial glow it draws the turtles toward the light, making them vulnerable to death from predation, vehicle traffic, and exhaustion or dehydration (International Dark, Practical Guide 2, 4). Many efforts are taken to preserve the remaining nesting grounds of sea turtles, but several hundred miles of coastline may be made unsuitable for nesting simply because of glaring lights from ocean-front condos, hotels, and strip malls.

An overabundance of street lights also has a noticeable effect on bats, drawing insects to the white-blue illumination, causing bats to swoop through the downcast light to catch them. It would be logical to assume that this would increase the number of bats in an area, but in many areas, this is having the opposite effect. According to a research review article, "The Dark Side of Light at Night", by Kristen Navara and Randy Nelson of the Institute for Behavioral Medicine Research at Ohio State University, certain species of bats that hunt by light easily out-compete other species that don't have that ability, driving those species out of large areas and pushing them one step closer to extinction. As an environmentalist and student of natural resources management, I have learned that wildlife population and biodiversity are often seen as key indicators of the health of an ecosystem, and a predictor of the viability of that system in the future. A decrease in biodiversity and wildlife populations is disturbing when careful planning and consideration can prevent species loss.

Another form of light pollution, urban sky glow, is defined by the IDA as "the brightening of the night sky over inhabited areas." This is an all too familiar occurrence for most people. At night we can spot a city along the horizon by sky glow alone. This increased ambient light has a striking effect on the predator-prey relationship in wildlife. According to Navara and Nelson, most prey are less likely to forage when the nights are brighter, naturally during the full moon, as a defense mechanism that ensures their survival. Dr. Harald Stark, a primary researcher for the National Oceanic and Atmospheric Administration, and the Cooperative Institute for Research on Environmental Science, states that the orange haze from urban sky-glow creates an environment that is at least twenty-five times brighter than the light of a full moon. When park lights and city glow make every night brighter, predators have an advantage, and easily pick off any nocturnal foragers (Navara and Nelson 220). This is a disadvantage both to prey and predator, and according to Resolution 516 of the American Medical Association, eventually decreases the populations of all nocturnal species. As prey is over-consumed, food becomes scarcer for the predator, causing both populations to decline.

Lighting has also been shown to affect the breeding habits of birds, fish, and mammals. In one early study, done in 1925 by W. Rowan, and reviewed by Navara and Nelson, birds that were kept in lighted outdoor cages lay eggs months early, despite nearly freezing Canadian temperatures. These birds were affected by light more than temperature, a fact that farmers have taken advantage of in brooding houses for decades, installing bright lights to encourage hens to lay more eggs during the darker months of winter (Navara and Nelson 220). Trout are similarly affected by light, spawning up to two months in advance when exposed to unnatural amounts of light (220). These effects on breeding timing can have detrimental effects on the population size of a species, significantly decreasing the chances that eggs will survive, further endangering the species.

The overwhelming brightness of urban sky glow also affects the migratory patterns of birds, insects and some aquatic species. Many species of nocturnally migrating birds are naturally drawn toward light, which is theorized to help during navigation (Navara and Nelson 221). Verlyn Klinkenborg, editor for the New York Times, in an article written for National Geographic entitled "Our Vanishing Night", writes about migrating birds that are drawn toward the orange glow from man-made cityscapes, stating "the effect is so powerful that scientists speak of songbirds and seabirds being 'captured' by searchlights... circling and circling in the thousands until they drop." When we consider the amount of light pollution in North America and Europe, the total possible effects on migrating birds is daunting.

Navara and Nelson list studies of other migrating animals that are also affected by light pollution, including monarch butterflies, silver eel, salmon, squid, and even zooplankton and shrimp. Squid fishermen take full advantage of the siren-like draw that light has on their prey, using an entire fleet to draw them in with enough light that they can be clearly seen from space (Klinkenborg). All of these examples, from migratory and mating problems, to problems in the predator-prey relationship show clearly that wildlife and its interaction with nature is not something that can be overlooked. Their lives literally revolve around the cycles of day and night. To change their environment and eliminate darkness puts them in unnecessary risk.

The effects on one animal in particular are of special importance to researchers. Humans are not so far removed from the natural environment as to escape similar effects to those seen in wildlife. Many diseases are being linked to exposure to light during the night, including cancer, heart disease, depression, infertility and obesity. All of these effects have a common connection, involving receptors in the retina of the eye, the circadian rhythm, and a chemical compound called melatonin (Navara and Nelson 216). Melatonin is formed in the pineal gland in the brain in response to darkness, when receptors in the retina receive no light. In dim light, such as would be found in a typical suburban or urban bedroom, melatonin levels are decreased by about fifty percent, and when the receptors in the eye are exposed to full-light, melatonin levels drop precipitously within an hour. Because melatonin is a trigger for other glands in the body, a drop in melatonin levels creates a drop in other chemicals, ones that are responsible for cell growth and repair, regulation of appetite and sleep, serotonin levels, and chemicals that help the body break down cholesterol and regulate blood pressure (Navara and Nelson 215-219). The American Medical Association affirms that light trespass is strongly suspected as a cause for lowered melatonin levels, depressed immune systems, and increased cancer rates. As much as our culture as a whole would argue man's triumph over nature through our technological advances, our species has existed as a part of nature since the beginning. Our bodies have adapted to natural conditions, including the cycle between day and night. To interrupt this cycle throws off every physiological system that depends on it.

The correlation between cancer and light pollution was introduced when data from a study of shift workers, as a sub-group in the longitudinal Nurses' Health Study, was reexamined by Eva S. Schernhammer, a Harvard University Epidemiologist in 2001. During the study, women nurses that worked third shift for an extended period of time were found to be at increased risk for breast cancer (Chepesiuk 26). In a follow-up study done in Israel, women who lived in areas where it was light enough to read a book outside at midnight were found to be 73-percent more likely to develop breast cancer than those living in areas with the least amount of outdoor lighting, even when confounding variables, such as population density, affluence, and air pollution were taken into account (27). Such a dramatic increase in cancer is startling, and the correlation with an overabundance of light gives a clearer understanding of why solving the problem of light pollution should be a priority.

Researchers have begun to design experiments to directly measure the effect of melatonin levels on tumors. In one such study, published in 2005 in the journal Cancer Research, tumors that were transplanted into rats grew at the same rate with injections of melatonin-deficient blood drawn from patients during the daytime and from patients whose blood was drawn after exposure to light at nighttime , but when injected with blood drawn during darkness, tumor growth slowed (Chepesiuk 26). In a similar study of deer mice in either natural day-night environment or constant-light, 90-percent of those that were exposed to constant light developed tumors, while mice in the other group, which had a natural day and night cycle, had none (Navara and Nelson 219). These findings could be dramatically important to our understanding of how the human body repairs itself during sleep, and lead in a new direction in the treatment and prevention of cancer. Furthermore, if melatonin has such a dramatic effect on a tumor, similar effects might also be seen in aging and general health.

Another concerning area of human health that is effected is infertility. A significant amount of research has been done on the effects of overexposure to light in small mammals, showing effects ranging from suspended estrous cycles in females, to lowered sperm counts in males, along with behavioral changes in the timing and efficiency of mating, decreasing reproduction (Navara and Nelson 220). Similar effects may be seen in the human body from drops in melatonin, which is shown to have a down-stream effect on several hormones in the human body, including reproductive, adrenal, and thyroid hormones (217). This could be a significant break-through in the treatment of infertility, as exposure to light could be managed along with other techniques used to increase fertility.

Despite the many complex consequences of light pollution, the solution is a fairly simple one. It's not nearly as complex as the solution to toxic waste, or mercury pollution, or carbon in the atmosphere. Many communities have already taken giant strides toward ending light pollution, and many other communities are considering their own plans. The International Dark-Sky Association puts forth several ideas that will effectively stop light pollution and the problems associated with it: shielded light fixtures, effective and purposeful placement of lights, and energy saving light curfews (International Dark, Practical Guide 1, 3).

Most light fixtures waste a considerable amount of the light they produce. Among the worst are globe-shaped pole lights, which cast most of their light into the sky, cause glare by shining light horizontally, and leave shadows along the ground. According to the National Park Service, 50-percent of light from a typical fixture shines upward, 10-percent causes glare, and about 40-percent is productive light (Chepesiuk 23). In fact, the United States wastes billions of dollars in unnecessary lighting, with an estimated additional 10 billion dollars in wasted energy from the use of un-shielded light fixtures (American Medical Association). This wasted energy is also responsible for contributing 14.7 million tons of carbon dioxide to our atmosphere (International Dark, Practical Guide 1, 3). In response to the problem, the International Dark-Sky Association has created a Fixture Seal of Approval program. According to David Penasa, of the International Dark-Sky Association, IDA approved, shielded lights cast light downward, at least fifteen degrees below horizontal, eliminating glare, light trespass, and wasted light and energy. By simply using this shielded design, a great deal of light pollution would be prevented, without denying the necessity of outdoor lighting.

Public knowledge of shielded fixtures is important because many out-door lighting fixtures are being replaced in favor of newer high-efficiency designs. In an open letter to dark-sky advocates, executive director of the International Dark Sky Association, Bob Parks, states that "it will be nearly impossible to overcome the tidal wave of development ... [but] we have a golden opportunity to exploit a once in a century paradigm shift in out-door lighting." Parks also states that through dialogue with industry lead-ers, most outdoor lighting is now using a shielded design. The American Medical Association, in resolution 516, supports light pollution reduction efforts, and suggests that all new outdoor lighting be fully shielded designs. With the current changes in outdoor lighting underway, advocates can encourage the right choices to ensure that any changes being made are not only energy efficient, but shielded to prevent light pollution.

Undoubtedly the most obvious solution to the light problem is to sim-ply reduce the total amount of outdoor lighting used. It would be difficult to argue against the fact that the United States has simply overused outdoor lighting, and cutting back to what is necessary and beneficial would be the quickest, easiest, and cheapest way to make a large impact on the problem of light pollution. Homeowners and city planners often put up outdoor lights for security and safety, without realizing that the human eye has great difficulty adjusting from intense light to darkness, and excess lighting actually leads to lowered visibility (International Dark, Practical Guide 1, 3). This affects nighttime driving, creating moments of lowered visibility while the eyes adjust to a sudden lighted area or to the next dark area beyond the lights. This also affects security issues for homeowners. While it seems logical that a porch light would increase the ability to see an intruder or trespasser, the light actually creates deep shadows beyond its reach that would normally be illuminated by the night sky (3).

The encouraging news about light pollution is that it has an inherently a grass-roots solution. No community has to wait on a federal government program to take action. We don't need large amounts of funding to trickle down to us in order to solve the problems associated with light pollution, and we don't need to wait until the EPA and congress agree to write their own laws. The immediate effects of light pollution can be reduced at the household level by turning off lights during the natural nighttime, and at the neighborhood level, the township level, and within greater metropolitan areas through lighting ordinances. If a large enough area enacted widespread changes to lighting policy, people and wildlife in that area would be free from the problems caused by light pollution.

According to Chepesiuk, "two-thirds of the U.S. population and more than one-half of the European population have already lost the ability to see the Milky Way with the naked eye." Nearly all Americans live in an area where sky brightness affects the ability to see the stars, which should nearly cover the sky above. In a culture pervaded by a compartmentalized and disconnected relationship to nature, the inability to see our own galaxy only furthers the disconnectedness. As we look to the sky at night, and can easily count the stars, we ought to wonder, exactly how much of all this artificial light is actually necessary and beneficial.

As our culture moves toward a more sustainable future, we should look toward ending light pollution as a starting goal. The simple solutions to the problem make it a proverbial low-hanging fruit, and offer a chance to significantly improve wildlife habitat and human health. When our children can again look to the sky, gaping in wide-eyed wonder at the stars, as innumerable as the grains of sand on a beach, we will have reached our goal to end light pollution, but more importantly we will have begun to reestablish the connection between ourselves and the natural environment.

Works Cited

American Medical Association. *Resolution 516: Advocating and Support for Light Pollution Control Efforts and Glare Reduction for Both Public Safety and Energy Savings.* 30 Mar. 2009. Print.

Chepesiuk, Ron. "Missing the Dark: Health Effects of Light Pollution." *Environmental Health Perspectives* 117.1 (Jan. 2009): A20-A27. Print.

"Edison's Lightbulb." *The Franklin Institute.* The Franklin Institute, n.d. Web. 27 Feb. 2011.

International Dark-Sky Association. *Practical Guide1: Introduction to Light Pollution.* Darksky.org, June 2009. Web.18 Feb. 2011.

---. *Practical Guide 2: Effects of Artificial Light at Night on Wildlife.* Darksky. org, 2008. Web. 18 Feb. 2011.

Klinkenborg, Verlyn. "Our Vanishing Night." *National Geographic* Nov. 2008: 102-123. *GreenFILE.* Web. 21 Feb. 2011.

Navara, Kristen, and Randy Nelson. "The Dark Side of Light at Night: Physiological, Epidemiological, and Ecological Consequences." *Journal of Pineal Research* 43.3 (Oct. 2007): 215-224. Print.

Parks, Bob. Open Letter to Dark Sky Advocates. n.d. *International Dark-Sky Association.* International Dark-Sky Association. Web. 21 Feb. 2011.

Penasa, David. "Getting Started with an Outdoor Lighting Ordinance." *International Dark-Sky Association.* International Dark-Sky Association, May 2002. Web. 21 Feb. 2011.

Stark, Harald. *Nitrate Radicals get Their Chance at Night.* Interview. BBC. n.d. Web. 28 Feb 2011.

Amanda Reed
Writing 150

Modeling the Sustainability Movement

Sustainability is the buzz-word of the twenty-first century. Nearly everyone, including the oil industry, is claiming to be "green". When our ideas about creating a sustainable future are defined by to-do lists, catch-phrases, and banned substances, it creates a set of standards that are easily manipulated and watered down into marketing schemes for the current unsustainable industrial model. The sustainability movement runs the very real threat of being absorbed into the industrial system without realizing any significant change. We don't need a slight twist to the old way of doing things. We need a new way of thinking, bold goals to guide our efforts, and the audacity to step forward and challenge the way we do things until our goals are met. GVSU offers a unique opportunity for students to accelerate the sustainability movement, through education, practice, and community involvement.

In order to define the sustainability movement we need a definition of sustainability that illustrates the end goals. Wendell Berry, in speaking of the organic movement in his book The Gift of Good Land, says "An organic farm, properly speaking, is not one that uses certain methods and substances and avoids others; it is a farm whose structure is formed in imitation of the structure of a natural system" (qtd. in Gardener). If we transform this idea to be used to define sustainability, we begin to see that a simple alteration to current processes won't work. Sustainability is not the use of certain methods and substances, nor is it a list of banned chemicals and activities. Sustainability is achieved in the imitation of nature. The end goal is to place humanity back into a harmonious relationship with nature. In order to achieve such a challenging goal, our culture has a long and arduous road ahead. As outlined by Anthony Cortese and William Mc-Donough, of the non-profit group Second Nature, in their article "Education for Sustainability: Accelerating the Transition to Sustainability through Higher Education", colleges and universities have a unique opportunity to teach the skills necessary to lead our culture through the upcoming paradigm shift. Grand Valley State University is poised at the leading edge of this paradigm shift, teaching the next generation of leaders, and modeling a sustainable community example for others to follow. As students, we have an important opportunity to learn, participate, and guide this sustainability movement.

Grand Valley has become a national leader in the sustainability movement. Kaplan College Guide 2009 named it one of the top twenty-five environmentally responsible and cutting-edge green colleges and universities in the nation, the only school in Michigan to have that honor (Waite, GVSU Joins). Grand Valley's commitment to sustainability goes far beyond theory and debate. According to the Sustainability Guide put out by the Sustainable Community Development Initiative, the university breaks down its efforts into four groups: education, student involvement, community engagement, and administration, dining, and facilities services. This is important because it directly mirrors the relationships to sustainability that society as a whole encounters: career, home life, and community. This is also the exact model outlined and promoted by Second Nature as the way to teach students sustainable practices in a fully integrated way (Cortese and McDonough 2). Bart Bartels, the program manager of the Sustainable Community Development Initiative states "For a long time, sustainability was about awareness raising. I think now it's about making an impact. Students would much rather get out there and do something than sit in a meeting and talk about doing something" (qtd. in Pulsinelli). GVSU offers students a chance to put theory and ideas into practice, with the real and honest goal of making the university completely sustainable.

The first key area of the sustainability initiative at Grand Valley is education, and GVSU has got it covered. According to the Sustainable Community Development Initiative's Sustainability Guide, thirteen percent of all student credit hours are in sustainability related courses, which now total more than two hundred (Grand Valley 8). From my own experience on campus, I know these course offerings span several departments and cover a broad range of topics, from the anthropology department's Culture and the Environment and liberal studies' The Idea of Nature, to Sustainable Business Management and Resource Economics. The university also offers degree programs related to sustainability, including natural resource management, and a liberal studies emphasis on sustainability, as well as minors in environmental studies, natural resources, and adventure travel, and certificate programs that will soon include business, engineering, public service, and computing (8). As broad as the course and program offerings are, a great deal of the educational experience at Grand Valley occurs outside the course catalog, especially for the topic of sustainability. The sustainability initiative has a new library guide, called the Green Library for Sustainability Resources, which contains current news, links to informative websites, suggested books, databases, and information on organizations on and off campus. Further opportunities for learning include lectures and presentations, informal meetings and discussions, and observation and direct involvement in sustainable practices on campus.

As students on a campus that is striving for sustainability, we have several opportunities to observe and participate in the day-to-day aspects of a sustainable system. From my personal experience as a freshman on campus, I had never seen a composting program like the one currently in place on campus. As a natural resources major with a keen interest in sustainable community development, I am encouraged by the concentration of LEED-certified buildings, permeable pavements, rain gardens, farmers markets, and recycling bins. Such a concentration of sustainable practices might seem unrealistic if we weren't living in them every day. In effect, the environment on campus is training us to become global citizens.

Student involvement is another important aspect of Grand Valley's movement toward sustainability. Several student groups work toward sustainability, and students are encouraged not only to participate, but to lead and propose new projects. The Student Sustainability Partnership helps bring together students from different groups and all across campus that are interested in sustainability issues and projects on campus (Waite, New Organization). Several students have used opportunities for research and hands-on learning on campus. The Lanthorn and the Sustainability Guide, and the Sustainable Community Development Initiative's webpage all have examples of student-led projects that have significantly contributed to Grand Valley's sustainability goals. Examples like the Grand Valley Community Garden, which is now the Sustainable Agriculture Project, a biodiesel project that converts cooking oil into fuel and a professor that is using the classroom to increase energy efficient insulation in the homes of Grand Rapids residents.

A large part of Grand Valley's commitment to sustainability is the use of LEED building guidelines in all new construction and major remodeling.

According to Grand Valley's Sustainability Guide, "LEED buildings use 30 percent less energy, 40 percent less water, and 75 percent less material than regular buildings." The use of LEED guidelines will continue with the Mary Idema Pew Library, which will seek platinum status, the highest level of certification (Pulsinelli). However, the university isn't only using LEED guidelines. GVSU is also participating in a pilot program called the Sustainable Sites Initiative, a program designed to "create voluntary national guidelines and performance benchmarks for sustainable land design, construction, and maintenance" (Waite, GVSU Joins). Proposed recreation fields to the west of the current soccer fields will include a designed wetland to manage storm water and provide water for irrigation (Waite, GVSU Joins). Landscape design is an important factor that, when paired with environmentally responsible building practices, will move Grand Valley toward its ultimate goal of complete sustainability.

Grand Valley's sustainability initiative is not simply education and discussion, or a set of feel-good volunteer activities and exhibited buildings to model sustainable principles. Grand Valley's end goal is complete sustainability by 2037 (Grand Valley 20). Each piece of the sustainability initiative is directed toward this goal. The downfall of all sustainability goals seems to be the perception of what is realistic. Especially when viewing the complete un-sustainability of our society, the goals of our movement seem completely unrealistic. But then again, so were the goals of the suffragettes, and those of the civil rights movement. Margaret Mead, famous anthropologist, convinced that the patterns of war, racism, and environmental exploitation are learned behaviors, says "Never doubt that a small group of thoughtful, committed citizens can change the world. Indeed, it is the only thing that ever has."

The sustainability movement has already begun on campus, and what is being done on campus is beginning to spread to the surrounding community. In the proverbial journey of a thousand steps, the first few have already been taken. We have a choice to participate, to push the bounds of the sustainability movement forward with our own efforts, or to sit idly by and let the opportunity pass. A wise Buddhist teacher and philosopher, Daisaku Ikeda says "No matter how complex global problems may seem, it is we ourselves who have given use to them. They cannot be beyond our power to resolve." The problems caused by environmental abuse, and the systems that support further degradation, are all human-made. These problems belong to us; we created them. We wield the power to break them, bend them, and destroy them. The past choices that led us to this point were made out of arrogant disunity with the cycles of nature. With hope and action, modeled by the community at Grand Valley, our current choices can undo the degradation and return our culture to an "organic" form of sustainability that benefits, and benefits from, nature.

Works Cited

Cortese, Anthony D., and William McDonough. "Education for Sustainability: Accelerating the Transition to Sustainability through Higher Education." *Environmental Grantmakers Association News & Updates,* Spring 2001: 11-14. Print.

Gardner, Levi. "Deep Organic: Agriculture for the 21st Century." *TEDx Grand Valley.* Grand Valley State University, 26 Oct. 2010. Web. 26 Mar. 2011.

Grand Valley State University. Sustainable Community Development Initiative. *Sustainability Guide.* Grand Valley State University Press. 2010. Print.

"GVSU Noted as 'Cutting-Edge Green' University." *GVNow.* Grand Valley State University, 6 Aug. 2008. Web. 26 Mar. 2011.

"Margaret Mead (1901-1978): An Anthropology of Human Freedom." *Intercultural Studies.org.* The Institute for Intercultural Studies. n.d. Web. 31 Mar. 2011.

Pulsinelli, Olivia. "Grand Valley State University STARS in Sustainability Efforts." *Business Review West Michigan.* 24 Mar. 2011. Web. 26 Mar. 2011.

Waite, Molly. "GVSU Joins Pilot Program for Sustainable Sites Initiative." *Grand Valley Lanthorn.* 19 July 2010. Web. 26 Mar. 2011.

---. "New Organization to Collaborate Student Sustainability Efforts." *Grand Valley Lanthorn.* 8 Apr. 2010. Web. 26 Mar. 2011.

Joseph Early
WRT 150

5.5lbs of Pressure

I was in paradise. I had never been on a cruise before, and the smell of the ocean engulfing the small country sized ship was majestic. There was a buffet of fresh seafood around every corner, and with the ship now in international waters, I could finally drink alcohol legally. I didn't even remember how I had gotten to this most perfect of places, but it hardly seemed to matter right now. My first order of business was the internal debate between swimming in the glimmering blue water on the upper deck pool or feasting upon the mountains of crab legs and lobster tails.

"Joe," I heard from somewhere. "Joe wake up, man."

No, I'm still in Iraq.

The small dusty room was still blurry from my luxurious hour long nap. My trusty sidekick, James, and I were on a twenty four hour radio detail, which meant we had to listen to our well rested comrades drive around on patrols. Our idea of switching on and off listening to the radio every hour sounded like such a good plan, up until this moment. It didn't matter now though, because this was the last hour of our shift.

I hoisted my body from the most uncomfortable cot ever made and looked at James and waited for him to inform me of what I had missed while I was away on my cruise. James was a poster board soldier, like the ones from the commercials; however, on this day his usually sharp military haircut somehow looked a mess, and his uniform was immersed with sweat from the morning heat. "Patrol one and two are inside the base eating," he mumbled, almost falling asleep.

"Gotcha. Everyone's eating except us," I grumbled back to him. "Anything else?"

"Yeah, the natives are getting restless," he quipped just before letting out a faint snore. Even sleep deprived James could still be sarcastic. It was one of many Islamic holidays, and we just so happened to be right down the road from the finish line of their long city to city voyage. The growing number of people arriving in the city over the past few days worried our commander about our safety, and it was likely that all patrols would stay on

---

Joseph wrote his portfolio in the class of Sister Lucia Treanor, F.S.E.

the base for a few days until the crowds dispersed. It was a shame, because there was nothing to do on the base. Our platoon of thirty two were the only Americans on the base, and the rest were Salvadorian and spoke little to no English.

The time kept ticking, and I continued to pointlessly listen to a radio with no one on the other end. It was only 11:15 a.m., so I still had about forty five minutes left to try to stay awake. I figured I would attempt to count the bullet holes that had pierced the paper thin mud walls again. It was an impossible task, but it forced me to stand up and walk around. Usually around five hundred I would give up and my hour would be close to over.

After counting for a few minutes, I began to hear yelling, but I couldn't make out what was being said. It grew in volume steadily as it got closer. It was only one voice, and now it sounded like it was inside our building. I still couldn't make anything out though. It sounded like a coyote had caught on fire and that the only way he could put it out was to scream miscellaneous high pitched sounds. I decided it would be a good idea to unholster the 9mm Berretta pistol that was attached to my right leg, just in case. The sound was moving rapidly in our direction. I leaned over to the cot and shook James awake. Just as he was about to ask why I was waking him up, the door to the room slammed open tossing pieces of the cheap wall in all directions. Any shred of drowsiness in either of us had also been tossed aside and replaced with the alertness of a hunting eagle ready to strike.

Bursting through the door was an out of control Salvadorian. His usually brown colored face was dark red like he was out of breath, but he was still yelling like a burnt coyote. He stopped just in front of us and continued his screeching rhapsody. The panic in his eyes informed me that something must be terribly wrong, but as for the words pouring from lips I had no clue. Knowing more Spanish than myself, James was able to break down what was being said, and the panic in the Salvadorians eyes had now transferred over to James' eyes. James said something in Spanish, and the high pitched Salvadorian ran off continuing to yell. James, still halfway lying on the couch, popped to his feet and, as calmly as I had ever heard him speak, said, "The front gate is being attacked." The panic shot to my eyes and rippled through my body like cold water rushing through my veins.

James and I stared at each other for what seemed like an hour, and then as though a director yelled "action," we both began playing our roles. I donned my bullet proof vest, which felt as if it was filled with feathers instead of the fifty pound metal plates that were actually inside. We grabbed our M16 rifles and left the room hastily. The door to the outside of the building was open, and it supplied the only light for us as James and I sprinted down the long hallway like bullets being fired from a gun.

We emerged from the building and continued straight for our humvee fifty yards away. The heat from the sun caused sweat to pour from my skin and my breath to quicken instantly. The rest of our platoon was in stride with us as they left running from the cafeteria. We had arrived at the humvees at the same time, and the only audible thing I could hear was our lieutenant instructing us to get to the front gate, as if he could make us move quicker then we already were.

I opened the two hundred pound bullet proof steel driver's door and plopped in the seat causing dust to fly into the air all around me. The impenetrable humvee had been heated by the afternoon sun, and it felt like I had jumped into an over worked oven on Thanksgiving Day. I placed my M16 on my lap and turned the ignition on the humvee to make our battle machine roar. I muscled the gear lever from park to drive and then looked at James in the passenger seat. "Let do this!" he shouted over the loud thundering of the engine.

In response, I slammed the gas pedal to the floor and continued to press harder, in hopes that I could make this five ton monster move quicker. The dust from the gravel road overran our vehicle until we reached the freshly paved one hundred yard long black top road that would lead us to the front gate.

I retrieved my M16 from my lap and a magazine of ammunition to load my weapon, a process that was like trying to drive while eating a cheeseburger and talking on the cell phone at the same time. Up ahead I could see dark earth being spit up as mortars impacted the ground. Surprisingly, the question, why am I driving towards all of this? never crossed my mind. Instead, a cool feeling washed over my body like someone was covering me with ice packs. I couldn't hear any of the explosions I was seeing, and all I could do was press even harder on the accelerator.

We approached the war zone that use to be the front gate, and I slammed on the breaks as hard as I had been pressing on the gas pedal, reminding both James and myself that we had forgotten to put on our seatbelts. I turned off the humvee and jumped out to the barbarous environment I had just been rushing towards.

I used the hood of the vehicle as cover from any bullets or mortar fragments that may head my way. James ran around the vehicle and crouched down next to me aiming his rifle towards an open area behind me, covering my back. Nothing had to be said.

I still couldn't hear any of the explosions that were dusting the air all around us, but squinting through the dense cloud of suspended dirt I could see a crowd of people shooting their automatic rifles at us. So, I steadied my M16 rifle on the hood of the humvee and peered through the sights. I could see everything clearly now.

My right thumb rotated my rifles selector switch from "safe" to "fire," and I placed my right index finger on the trigger. I aimed my rifle at the impending threat, and the only thing I could feel or hear was my heart pounding. Surely had I not been wearing my bullet proof vest it would have burst from my chest.

At that moment someone pressed pause on everything except me, and my brain sent a memo down my right arm to my index finger. This message was for my finger to apply 5.5 pounds of pressure to the trigger, which released a spring loaded "hammer" to strike the end of the firing pin. The firing pin hit the blasting cap of the bullet resting in the barrel of my rifle, which ignited the black powder inside the bullet. This powerful explosion roused the copper projectile and started it on its one hundred meter journey. The groves in the barrel of the rifle caused the copper projectile to spin as it escaped the control of my rifle. The pressure from the round leaving my barrel forced the bolt of my rifle to slide backwards towards my shoulder. As the bolt moved backwards it simultaneously discarded the hot brass container and spring loaded the "hammer" again. The bolt then reached a large spring, which forced the bolt to travel away from my shoulder and back towards the barrel. In moving forward, the head of the bolt grasped another bullet from the magazine of ammunition and cleanly placed it into the barrel of my rifle. My rifle was now reloaded and ready to fire again, even before the copper projectile had had a chance to reach the end of the path I had just sent it on. Lord have mercy on my soul.

It seemed like only minutes had passed as the sun retreated from the sky. My shoulder ached from the constant recoil from my rifle. In all, eight hours had passed, and finally everything was quiet. We had fired so many rounds of ammunition that a helicopter had to make several ammo drops to our small circle of humvees throughout the day, and the empty brass cartridges that had replaced the sand all around us reflected this fact. I couldn't recall exactly what had just happened, and I looked over to James to help me find the answer. His face was covered in black, and his tired eyes seemed to be asking me the same thing.

We got back into our sweltering humvee and drove quietly back to our building in disbelief over what had just transpired. When we returned to the building we walked into the large open bay sleeping area, which housed all thirty two of us. I found my cot and peeled my sopping wet clothing from my sore body and replaced them with fresh sleeping clothes. I wish it was a shower day. After being up for 36 hours and fighting for 8 of them, the adrenaline was finally flushed from my system. I had just fired thousands of rounds of ammunition, maybe killed several people, and almost died myself.

Little did I know that years later, after receiving my "Here's how to write a resume" pamphlet from the Army, that normal everyday life problems wouldn't really bother me. Instead, being in large crowds of people, hearing footsteps behind me, and loud startling noises would be my everyday life problems. For better or worse this day would change my life forever, but at that moment I didn't care about years down the road. All I wanted was to get back to my cruise.

Joseph Early
WRT 150

Social and Media Influences on
the "Support the Troops" Campaign

Shortly after the invasion of Iraq, shouts of "Support the Troops" could be heard ringing from home to home across the nation. Whether it be a simple "thank you" and a hand shake or an elaborate parade, this "Support the Troops" rhetoric is not new. In fact, it dates back to the beginning of our great country. However, in modern history our society has accepted returning veterans differently under a variety of circumstances. Almost everyone in my family is a veteran, including myself, and we have veterans from every war from World War II to current, even the Grenada War. In asking my family members about their return from their overseas deployments, all of them said that veterans returning from the Vietnam War had it the worst. My uncle Mark, a Vietnam veteran, stated that he was treated as an outcast from society, even from his own mother, when he returned from combat. He was shunned by the community he had grown up in and stayed confined to his room for most of the day. In contrast, my mother, father, and other uncles stated that they were treated to the open arms of family and friends upon their return.

While serving my first combat tour in Iraq in 2004, I would sometimes think about how we would be accepted back into society. Would I be shunned by my community and destined to be incarcerated in my bedroom or welcomed home in a friendly manner? Luckily, my homecoming experience was a feeling of warmth and happiness and greeted with a marching band, friends, and family as we disembarked the aircraft. While proudly walking around the airport, strangers seemed to feel compelled to walk up to us to shake our hands or offer to buy us a beer.

As I went on to serve my second and third deployments to Iraq, the public support for the Iraq War decreased dramatically. There were protests calling for the withdrawal of troops from Iraq saying, "No blood for oil," "How many lives per gallon?," and "Read my lips: No war in Iraq." With these protests and public support for the Iraq War declining, it reminded me of how my family had described the public's reactions to the Vietnam War, and I wondered whether I would still be welcomed back as kindly as I had been the first time. Fortunately, I was, and it seemed as though each time I stepped off the plane from a deployment, the warmth was warmer and the welcome home even stronger.

How could it be that society had changed its opinion of the Iraq War, but acceptance of returning veterans had increased? Why was I not treated like a returning Vietnam veteran, when their war was so strongly criticized by many as well?

One answer might be that, since the Vietnam War, we as a nation have "socialized ourselves to be patriotic" and now support the people fighting in the name of our country (Coy, Woehrle, and Maney 171). Meaning that people felt ashamed of the treatment of returning Vietnam veterans, even if they had not personally treated them in a negative matter, that they changed the way they act and the way they teach their children to act towards returning veterans. This answer seems to make sense, but it does not seem to describe fully the growing intensity of our nation's support for the troops. As our troops were serving in Afghanistan, about two years before the invasion of Iraq, we did indeed show support for our troops, but not nearly so intensely as for the Iraq War troops. It seemed as though many had forgotten that there was even a war in Afghanistan altogether, and returning veterans from Afghanistan were assumed to be Iraq veterans by a large majority of the public. I have found that there were two major factors that, by an unplanned sequence of events, meshed together to form our current "Support the Troops" campaign: the media and peace activists.

Outlining the impact of the media, assistant professor of sociology at Concordia College Andrew M. Linder points out that war coverage has not only changed with the advancement of technology and transportation, but also with how the Department of Defense has allowed the media to perceive military conflicts. The Vietnam War offered journalists to roam freely, and they were granted access to Vietnam civilians and military sources throughout the war at any given time. This reporting allowed the media to report more on the effects and outcomes of the war. In contrast, Gulf War journalists were escorted by military personal everywhere and allowed limited access off of the bases. This forced the media to report mainly on the troops' feelings and life style (26).

As professors of sociology Patrick Coy, Lynne Woehrle, and Gregory Maney note, during all these wars there were peace activists who were helping to direct the media's coverage and public opinion, and also attempting to garner support for their anti-war cause within the nation (171). As known from history, those peace activists succeeded with the Vietnam War as their anti-war goal swept the nation. With the Gulf War, it would seem that they were largely unsuccessful, until the U.S. pulled troops from Iraq quickly, allowing media organizations free range to talk to civilians. Although the media and the peace activists are not working with each other, they do seem to be connected in some way, and depending on that connection, are able to shape public opinion.

Undoubtedly learning from these previous wars, the Department of Defense enacted the Media Embedded Program in mid-2002 through the Public Affairs Office in anticipation of the invasion of Iraq. "The Office of the Secretary of Defense Public Affairs concept for Operation Iraqi Freedom had three objectives: dominate the media coverage of the war, counter third-party disinformation, and assist in garnering U.S. public and international support. The Embedded Media Program assisted in the accomplishment of the objectives" (Wright S-6). Richard K. Wright of the Institute for Defense Analyses also shows that, of all the journalists in Iraq, approximately two thirds (692) were part of the Embedded Media Program (S-3); embedded journalists represented 244 media organizations and accounting for 64 percent of the national/regional media coverage, 27 percent of the international media coverage, and nine percent of the local media coverage (S-3).

The Department of Defense made the Embedded Media Program very enticing to media organizations. Linder found that it would cost a media outlet around $10,000 a month to keep a journalist in Iraq, but "through the Embedded Media Program it only cost a fraction of that cost" (42). The Embeds were given camouflage uniforms, food, and a military unit to travel with, and they were sent to the military units 7-10 days before the invasion of Iraq began. This allowed journalists to get to know the troops within the military unit they would be traveling with and give them a real time view of the invasion (42). In addition, the military service branches also conducted a one-week Media Training Course prior to meeting the units they would be traveling with. Wright points out that "the purpose of the course was to allow participating news personnel to gain basic military knowledge and build skills that [would] help them safely and accurately report on joint military operations" (V-38). With approximately 17 brigades, consisting of 108,964 military personnel from all branches of service the embedded media were stretched far and wide to cover the Iraq War on several U.S. ships and with U.S. military ground forces (Carter CRS.1).

When the invasion of Iraq began in 2003, Linder found that several of the embedded media personnel began sending out troop-centered reports instead of reporting on the outcomes of the Iraq War itself. He even found that many critics claimed that embedded journalists had succumbed to "Stockholm Syndrome," describing how embedded journalists began reporting from the "view of the troops that were protecting them" and focusing on the hardships of the troops instead of the outcomes of the war (23). On the other hand, being embedded allowed the media to report more accurately on what the troops were doing. One example came from Ryan Chilcote of CNN:

> It is still a place where soldiers, when they pass through, are very apprehensive. A soldier was telling me that every time he goes through Mahmudiya, he takes his weapon off safety so he's ready for any eventuality....As [the soldiers] attempt to establish order and bring a little bit of normalcy back into life in southern Baghdad, they're finding themselves in more and more of a peacekeeping role. But still it's a matter of resources, and they have to transition from going through all of the buildings, all of the regions in southern Baghdad, to the peacekeeping operation. (April 14, 2003)

This report not only depicts some of the emotions I felt when I was in Iraq, but it also accurately describes the difficult transition from war to peacekeeping for soldiers. He is able to report that the soldiers are transitioning to a peacekeeping role, but are still on guard for a war role should the occasion arise; a view that would possibly be missed by an un-embedded journalist. However, despite this example, Linder found that most embedded journalists became more like activists for the troops. He points out that "[embedded journalists] spent six weeks wearing chemical suits, sweating in six-man tanks, and taking cover from enemy fire as part of an invading force and living as hard as the troops" (24).

Two examples from The New York Times, from around the same period show the contrast in reporting from an embedded and an un-embedded journalist's point-of-view; both journalists are from the same media organization. First the un-embedded journalist, Friedman, reports:

> Um Qasr was the first town liberated by coalition forces. But 20 days into the war, it is without running water, security or adequate supplies. I went in with a Kuwaiti relief team, who, taking pity on the Iraqis, tossed out extra food from a bus window as we left. The Umm Qasr townsfolk scrambled after the food like pigeons jostling for bread crumbs in a park. This was a scene of humiliation, not liberation. We must do better. (April 9, 2003)

In contrast, the embedded journalist, Dwyer, writes:

> [Colonel Gibbs] had come well stocked with baby wipes and the essentials of living without running water, with no showers or regular toilets....Clothing turns out not to be all that important a part of the kit, since the protective chemical suits have to be worn 24 hours a day. Most of the soldiers wear just a T-shirt and underwear. (March 26, 2003)

According to Linder, the American public was two thirds more likely to read about articles like Dwyer's, the hardships and hygiene habits of the troops, than they were Friedman's, the outcome of the war.

Away from the war physically, there were voices screaming in the United States; as Coy, Woehrle, and Maney describe, Peace Movement Organizations (PMOs) had put together an "unusually well organized campaign" (17). These PMOs were effectively able to use the media reports from embedded journalists to make claims that the troops did not have enough training, the right type of equipment, and that deployments were arbitrarily being extended; the PMOs placed the blame on the government and military institutions for forcing troops to "fight with one hand behind their back" (Coy, Woehrle, and Maney 17).

As the Iraq War waged on, public opinion polls showed that the support for the Iraq War dropped significantly (Berinsky and Druckman 130); but as we can still see today, our support for the troops has only increased. Possibly still in shock from their new found success, even PMOs shied away from publicly singling out troops in a negative manner. Coy, Woehrle, and Maney show that during the Abu Ghraib torture reports, most PMOs called the incidents "horrific," but focused on blaming the Bush Administration instead of the individual troops who had committed the crimes. The only larger organization that insisted on prison time for individual soldiers guilty of torture was the Council on American-Islamic Relations (CAIR). In fact, CAIR accounts for 75 percent of the negative troop rhetoric coming from the PMOs, but only a fraction of the overall voice of PMOs (182). Since CAIR is such a small voice, when compared to the rest of the PMO's, media, and "American Patriots," CAIR's views are seldom heard.

Whether it was intended or not, the media's coverage at the beginning of the war, assisted by the Department of Defense's Embedded Media Program, flooded the U.S. with empathetic and troop-centered reports. The PMOs were then able to intensify the public's reaction using these media reports as ammunition to call for support for the troops while being able to achieve their goal of driving down support for the Iraq War. For the first time, peace activists and "American Patriots" finally had one thing they could agree on, "Support the Troops."

Works Cited

Berinsky, Adam J., and James N. Druckman "The Polls-Review: Public opinion research and support for the Iraq War." *Public Opinion Quarterly* 71.1 (2007): 126-141. *Oxford Journals.* Web. 30 Jan. 2011.

Carter, Linwood B. "Iraq: Summary of U.S. Forces." *CRS Report For Congress* (2005): CRS 1-CRS 11. *Defense Technical Information Center.* Web. 30 Jan. 2011.

Chilcote, Ryan. Interview by Anderson Cooper. *On the Scene.* CNN. 14 Apr. 2003. Mahmudiya, Iraq, 30 Jan. 2011. Web. Transcript.

Coy, Patrick G., Lynne M. Woehrle, and Gregory M. Maney "Discursive Legacies: The U.S. Peace Movement and 'Support the Troops.'" *Social Problems* 55.2 (2008): 161-189. *JSTOR.* Web. 30 Jan. 2011.

Dwyer, Jim. "Troops Endure Blowing Sands and Mud Rain." *New York Times* 26 Mar. 2003: B4. Web. 30 Jan. 2011.

Friedman, Thomas L. "Hold your Applause." *New York Times* 9 Apr. 2003. Web.

Linder, Andrew M. "Among the Troops: Seeing the Iraq War through Three Journalistic Vantage Points." *Social Problems* 56.1 (2009): 21-48. *JSTOR.* Web. 30 Jan. 2011.

Wright, Richard K. "Assessment of the DoD Embedded Media Program" *Institute for Defense Analysis* (Sep. 2004): S1-K5. *Defense Technical Information Center.* Web. 30 Jan. 2011.

Joseph Early
WRT 150

The Opera

The opera L'enfant et les sortilèges: Fantaisie lyrique en deux parties
(The Child and the Spells: A Lyric Fantasy in Two Parts), by Maurice
Ravel, is about the transformation of a misbehaved child who, through being shown the damage he has done to his surroundings and environment,
changes the manner in which he acts. The story is set in Normandy, France
and begins with a boy who does not want to do his homework. His mother
punishes him and tells him to stay in his room until dinner. After she
leaves, the boy begins to wreak havoc and destroy everything in the room.
Then the furniture, fire, and even his homework come to life and begin to
frighten him until he passes out and awakes in a forest. There he is con-
fronted and attacked by the trees he cut and the animals he tortured. In the
confrontation, a squirrel gets injured, and the boy helps heal it, after which
he becomes unconscious from his injuries. Through the act of kindness of
helping the squirrel, the animals feel that the boy has learned his lesson and
carry him back to the safety of his home.

The Grand Valley State University's Opera House, in conjunction with
the Grand Rapids Ballet Companies showing of the Mother Goose Suite,
performed a rendition of L'enfant et les sortilèges. Some of the interesting
aspects of the performance were the music, performance and costumes.

The lyrics were written in French and then translated into English, and
because they were translated, the words did not always seem to fit the bril-
liant sounds coming from the four man orchestra, nevertheless the audience could sense the emotions which it should be feeling by the rhythm
alone. Wondering why anyone would remove the beautiful foreign words,
which had the pleasure of being joined with such wonderful music, I
looked around at the audience. The performance was geared towards children no older than ten. How could the performers draw such impression-
able minds into the art, if the youth did not understand what was being
said? After all, the words of Big Bird and Elmo are still fresh in their minds.
Although the possibly flawless French words were changed, it was still a
wonderful display of sounds, and I believe the spirit of the music lived in
our young ones and myself.

The performance of some of the characters, on the other hand, did not give life to the story so much as the music. I was left with several children around me asking their bewildered parents why something was occurring or even what was occurring. With the music sung beautifully, even in English, I did not expect explanations; however, at times, I too, was wondering what was actually happening on stage. When furniture began to come to life, towards the end of act one, I could not understand why there was a tea pot and a china cup singing. Do not get me wrong, the section in which the tea pot and china cup sang and danced was beautiful, so beautiful, in fact, that the entire audience put the opera to an abrupt halt so the clapping of our hands could be heard throughout the building, but I still do not know why they were singing in the first place. Then there was an old guy and a bunch of numbers. If you had seen this opera with me, that last sentence would make sense. Out of nowhere the set changed, and dancing numbers with an old teacher emerged and began singing and moving around. The young boy danced in a way that did not fit in with the dancing numbers, but why were there dancing numbers? Well, they might have represented his homework, which he does not understand, because he will not study.

In contrast, a point in which the opera made clear, through acting and music, was when the boy helped the squirrel. Dr. May V. Seagoe, a former professor at the Graduate School of Education at UCLA, notes that a performance should give children a sense of adventure, allowing them to learn creatively good behavior and develop the concept of right and wrong (233). The tone of the music and the acting of the boy clearly showed that the boy had changed his misbehaving ways, by helping the squirrel he had once tortured, which, hopefully, guided the attending youth down the path of good morality.

Now, I can picture a person dressed as a cat, bug, or frog, but never in my life did I believe that my favorite costume from a live show would be two chairs. The top of the chairs were the performers heads, and the legs were their legs. They were encompassed by a frame, which resembled a recliner. For me, it was an original design which over shadowed the excellent and detailed costumes of the other cast members, barring the firefly. The firefly, which had a musical number dedicated to her, was dressed in a full body rainbow, fleece suit. The bright rainbow color detracted from the wings and what remained was a rainbow suit dancing around. If it were not for the actual sign of a firefly which she was holding above her head during the song, I do not believe that I would have been able to tell it was a firefly. However, in current television programs aimed towards children, bright colors are used to attract the attention. I sense that, if polled, I may be in the minority in the judgment of the firefly's costume. The children seemed to enjoy the brightly colored firefly, so my opinion on that aspect is in the minority.

After walking out of the theater, I found myself making several judgments regarding the performance, some of which made it to what you just read. However, in pondering about who this opera was preformed for, I was able to see and appreciate its value. This opera was not crafted for me; it was shaped for the youth of our nation, the youth of the art, the youth of the attending audience. Dr. Wolfgang Schneider, a former Director of the Children's and Young People's Theatre Centre and lecturer at the Institute for Research on Literature for Young People, suggests that, sometimes, the only true criteria adults should use to critique a performance intended for children are their "rosy cheeks" and "shining eyes" (75). While I can make my assumptions about what I believe should or could have been better, it does not really matter. The smiles from the children leaving the performance made it obvious that not only was the message of the opera clear, but that the opera itself reached its intended purpose, to the intended audience, and with its intended success.

Works Cited

L'enfant et les sortilèges: Fantaisie lyrique en deux parties. By Maurice Ravel. GVSU Louis Armstrong Theatre, Allendale, Michigan. 25 Feb. 2011. Performance.

Schneider, Wolfgang. "'Rosy Cheeks' and 'Shining Eyes' as Criteria in Children's Theater Criticism." *The Lion and the Unicorn.* 19.1 (1995): 71-76. *Project MUSE.* Web. 21 Feb. 2011.

Seagoe, May V. "Issues and Criteria for Children's Television." *Educational Theatre Journal.* 4.3 (1952): 231-237. *JSTOR.* Web. 21 Feb. 2011.

Leslie Kuhn
WRT 150

One Man's Trash

I can recall numerous expeditions in which my mother would quite literally drag me along on her weekly garage sale shopping spree. She would scour house after house in search of what seemed to me as junk. Much to my dad's dismay, she would return home with rusty chairs, broken bed frames, vintage clothing, and one time even a bathroom sink. Each reclaimed item would soon become her masterpiece. She would refurbish and recycle her thrifty finds, and they would be as good as new. Despite my weekend frustrations with her as a child, I can now see the practicality and ingenuity behind her recycled purchases. Evidently, others caught on to this growing trend as well, and in contrast to the expanding technological and modern community, old fashion thrift shopping is becoming more popular than ever, especially in the fashion industry.

An everyday bargain and mystery allures adventurous customers to thrift shops and resale outlets. These stores offer the lowest prices around when it comes to discount clothing and accessories (Bass). Despite the hassle of sorting through racks and racks in search of a unique and thrifty piece, the prices for that piece are simply unbeatable. With over 18,000 thrift stores in the United States alone, and the current economic downturn these stores are bound to be successful (Christiansen). Unlike other stores, thrift stores are constantly changing. Consumers such as myself are attracted to the bargains and the adventure of a good deal. According to a 2008 study by the St. Claire - Association of Resale and Thrift Shops, thrift and resale stores have become one of the fastest growing retail industry, and in fact, resale has had a growth rate of five percent per year in the last three consecutive years, and for a good reason (Youssef). Consumers are finally acknowledging the benefits of resale shopping, and shopping at such stores is no longer considered a taboo. Many regard thrift shopping as savvy, chic, and environmentally friendly.

Thrift shopping at garage sales and flea markets is growing in popularity not only for college students, but also for adults, especially during this period of economic recession. It is apparent that thrift shopping is the "in" thing to do, and thrifty purchases are becoming increasingly socially

---

Leslie wrote her portfolio in the class of Professor Dauvan Mulally.

acceptable. Times have changed, and shoppers are not ashamed to admit to their thrift store purchases. In fact, many resale store shoppers brag about their thrifty purchases, and they are excited to have snagged a great deal that others may have quickly overlooked (Balfour). There are many worthwhile bargains for those who are willing to devote the time. While thrift shopping was frequently associated with individuals of lower income, nowadays thrifts shopping appeals to a large number of consumers from varying economic backgrounds (Christiansen). In fact, most of the resale shoppers are middle to upper-middle class bargain hunters (Rettig). Shopping places such as Goodwill, garage sales, flea markets, and second hand stores appeal to numerous demographics. In past experiences with thrift shopping, I have encountered people from all different backgrounds and walks of life, and nowadays thrift stores are always busy and bustling.

What attracts consumers to thrift shops differs based on each consumer's needs and desires, but it is apparent that growing thrift craze is partially fueled by society's desire for instant gratification and guilt-free buying. One could purchase five or six articles of clothing at a resale shop for the price of one article at a brand name store. According to Cindy Graham, Goodwill Industry's vice president of marketing in Central Indiana, Goodwill is one of the few places that you can find a tee shirt for 1.99 and jeans for 2.99 (Rettig). Many times these resale articles are eclectic and have more character than items purchased directly from large clothing corporations. Fashion editor, Debra Bass said, "On a good day, you can walk out with a bag full of items for less than the price of a Banana Republic tee shirt." A buyer feels no regrets after making a thrift store purchase, and more often than not the buyer feels that the purchase was justifiable due to its low prices and stylish practicality. In my own thrift experiences, I have been able to purchase four or five dresses, a pair of used red pumps, and several stylish tops for significantly less than the price of a pair of Hollister Jeans or an Abercrombie sweatshirt. Thrift shops offer a variety of clothing options for each fashion sense, and it appeals to both men and women who enjoy the thrill of creating a thrifty and personalized wardrobe.

It is evident that during a time of economic uncertainty, customers are searching for the best bang for their buck. Resale stores have noticed shoppers altering their purchases due to the economic crunch (Youssef). Ken Dalto, a retail analyst, claims that within the "thrifting business" there has been a "big boom" and " it is becoming a big business" (Youssef). The success of retail stores undoubtedly is at least partially due to the downfall of the market. Dan Ariely, a behavioral economist at Duke University claims that "thriftiness has become a habit, rather than a conscious decision" (Koven). Consumer trends are suggesting an era of penny saving frugality (Koven). Budget conscious consumers are getting creative with how they spend their money and how they shop for thrift clothing. Winne Lee, associate photo editor at Budget Living Magazine said, "If you're not afraid to dig deep and get really creative, then you can find something really cheap to repurpose" (qtd.in Tavitas). Evidently, consumers are stretching their dollars and using them in both creative and thrifty ways.

Whether it be because of the economic recession or an altered mind-set among consumers, thrift and resale shops continue to thrive. By purchasing resale clothing, there is no additional production, transportation, or work needed. Many consumers consider their thrift shopping to be a contribution to the battle against consumerism (Tavitas). Less clothes go to waste and more are re-purposed and given new life. It is easy to forget about the environmental impact that is associated with each new article of clothing. Each piece has to be manufactured, transported, and then sold at an inflated price. Additionally, by purchasing used clothing, the need for raw material is eliminated. Consequently, recycled purchases keeps products that have already been produced in circulation (Sohrabji). Thrifts stores cultivate recycled purchases of all kinds, and thus reducing the environmental impact and carbon footprints.

Though resale shopping serves to better the environment, it is also advantageous for all parties involved. Many times thrift store buyers overlook the impact that their shopping has on others. Purchasing through resale shops may directly benefit the lives of the poor or homeless. Goodwill Incorporated spent 83 percent of its total revenue on programs benefiting those who are unemployed, homeless, or suffering because of economic insufficiency. Additionally, Goodwill provides employment and support to those faced with similar dilemmas. In fact, during 2009 1.9 million people were served through employment of training programs ("Our Mission").Many other resale stores also employ and serve the local community through revenue and programs. Consequently, thrift shoppers of all kinds not only receive the benefit of a good deal, but they also receive the satisfaction of knowing that their purchase will improve the lives of others within their own community.

Despite the advances of an era of growing modern styles and technologies, thrift and resale stores are significantly prospering. Lower prices and creative touches, and endless inventory give resale stores a leg up on overpriced new fashion merchandise. Thrift shopping has proved to be a benefit of the economic recession as many shoppers save money, recycle, and provide for their community. As a daughter and a consumer, I applaud my mother's thrifty tendencies, and I aspire to follow in her footsteps and change the way other consumers look at resale stores and the ways that they spend their dollars.

Works Cited

Balfour, Barbara. "Recycling Fashion: Thrift Shopping Hotter than Ever." *North Bay Nugget* (2004): D.8. *LexisNexis Academic*. Web. 18 Mar. 2011

Bass, Debra. "Get a Thrill by Thrift Shopping." *St. Louis Post-Dispatch* (2008): 28. *LexisNexis Academic*. Web. 20 Mar. 2011.

Christiansen, Tim. "Information Sources for Thrift Shopping: Is There a 'Thrift Maven?'" *The Journal of Consumer Marketing*. 22.6 (2005): 323-31. *ABI/INFORM Global*. Web. 18 Mar. 2011.

Koven, Peter. "The New Thrift." *National Post* (2009): FP.7. *LexisNexis Academic*. Web. 20 Mar. 2011.

"Our Mission." *Goodwill.org*. Goodwill Industries, 2009. Web. 23 Mar. 2011.

Rettig, Ellen. "Middle Class Drives Thrift Stores." *Indianapolis Business Journal 19.3 (1998)*: 3. *LexisNexis Academic*. Web. 20 Mar. 2011.

Sohrabji, Sunita. "Conscious Fashionistas Promote Eco-Friendly Used Clothing." *India West* 34.25 (2009): B9. *Ethnic News Watch*. Web. 18 Mar. 2011.

Tavitas-Williams, Jeanie. "Beyond Thrift:: Resale Shops Appeal to EcoAware." *San Antonio Express News* (2004). *LexisNexis Academic*. Web. 18 Mar. 2011.

Youssef, Jennifer. "It's Boom Time for Area Thrift Stores." *Detroit News* (2008): A-1. *NewsBank*. Web. 18 Mar. 2011.

Leslie Kuhn
WRT 150

A *Growing* Industry and a Michigan Experience

Folk music blasts from underneath a nearby white canopy, and young and old alike adorn peculiar headbands with slender vegetables attached to the front. It is springtime, and farmers and local consumers alike celebrate the return of their much beloved crop. It's asparagus season in Western Michigan, and this calls for a celebration of epic proportions, well maybe not epic proportions, but it is a celebration nonetheless. A green parade consisting of about twenty people circles the small downtown village of empire, approximately ten times before eventually retiring to enjoy the rest of the Empire Asparagus Festival. Underneath the numerous tents local vendors serve a variety of delectable treats including asparagus ice cream, "asparagus dogs," asparagus beer, and much more. Just off the shores of the beautiful Lake Michigan, the small town of Empire cultivates the ideal atmosphere for this rather comical vegetable. The quirky festival held in Empire, is just one of the multiple asparagus festivals in Michigan, but many Michiganders are unaware of the success of their asparagus growing neighbors. It is asparagus time of year, and it is about time that this beloved vegetable receives some of the recognition it deserves.

The apparent popularity of the asparagus festival in Northern Michigan, leads one to assume that the Michigan asparagus industry is booming. That it is and, in fact, according to the Michigan Asparagus Advisory board, Michigan ranks third in the nation for their profitable asparagus production (Facts). Local farmers are reaping the benefits of their seasonal harvest, and their humble industry quietly keeps money within the local Michigan economy. These local harvesters rake in an annual total of 15,000,000 dollars from their asparagus crops (Facts). Little known to the rest of the community, the months of May and June are exceptionally busy times for Michigan asparagus growers. They are busy harvesting about 11,000 acres of fresh asparagus to be processed or sold at local vendors (Facts). The cities Empire and Oceana, Michigan are hosts to annual asparagus festivals, which honor the efforts of our local vegetable growers and families. It seems that Michigan asparagus growers are just as humble and down to earth as their precious crop. Many of the growers are family businesses passing their crops from generation to generation (Daelemans). The small town vibe and local connections provide a comfortable and simplistic atmosphere to host a modest festival for a seemingly modest vegetable.

While zany festivals such as the asparagus festivals do not boast their economic success, their products evidently speak for themselves. This somewhat laughable vegetable is not lacking in delicious flavor or essential nutrients, especially the top-notch Michigan asparagus. Michigan asparagus is home grown, and the short distance from the harvest to the dinner table makes Michigan asparagus extra tender and flavorful (Daelemans). Michigan growers are grateful for their local support, even Mitch Irwin, the director of the Michigan Department of Agriculture can not help but comment on this under appreciated vegetable. Irwin states, "You can't beat fresh Michigan asparagus for taste, quality and nutrition. By buying locally grown asparagus, you keep $65 million right here in Michigan supporting Michigan farmers, our rural communities, and our state's economy" (Lipe). As Irwin stated, Michigan asparagus is known for being a step above the rest. Michigan asparagus is both economically beneficial as well as nutritionally healthy. In fact, the local asparagus contains no fat, and it is a low sodium and calorie vegetable (Lipe). These nutritional and economic benefits may be a bore in comparison to other more interesting vegetable facts, but the numerous asparagus entrees are anything but mundane. The asparagus festivals of Empire and Oceana Michigan deliver a variety of asparagus themed dishes including, asparagus ice cream, asparagus crepes, pickled asparagus, deep fried asparagus and much more (Ward). It is no doubt that the Michigan Asparagus Industry is flourishing and profiting due to the creative use of the asparagus vegetable as well as the success of the festivals themselves.

While the popularity of the asparagus festivals and the industry itself seems to be growing, it seems that these small town festivals are often overshadowed by the popularity of larger and more commercial festivals such as the Cherry Festival in Traverse City. Although the Traverse City Cherry Festival is an annual tradition and a unique Michigan festival, it has become commercialized, and it has lost much of its hometown touch. Crowds of tourists from all over the state flock to the beaches of Traverse City to reserve their spot on the overpopulated beaches. Although these tourists rake in money for the Traverse City economy and local business owners, the tourists are no longer paying for an authentic experience. Over-priced food and tacky carnival rides may be attractive to some Michiganders, but for many others the rustic and unorthodox festivals, such as the Asparagus Festival, are more appealing.

Despite the popularity of the larger festivals, the Oceana Asparagus festival seems to be giving the National Cherry Festival a run for its money. In fact, Oceana, Michigan is known as the National Asparagus Capital, and it is host to the National Asparagus Festival (National). Although this festival is growing in size and popularity, it has not lost its small town charm. The National Asparagus Festival is held in Oceana County, and the location of the festival alternates between the towns of Hart and Shelby (National). These two towns provide Michigan with the greatest volume of asparagus production, and thus the title "Asparagus Capital" suits them (Facts). Every June within the Asparagus Capital, a number of asparagus related activities are held. These activities include an Asparagus arts and crafts fair, a 5K run, an asparagus parade, and an asparagus food show (National). The fun filled events and growing popularity of the Oceana Asparagus Festival are becoming comparable to that of the National Cherry Festival, and it is evident that much of their success is due to the seemingly small town vibe and bizarre asparagus entrees and events.

In contrast, the Empire asparagus festival, while not as grand, offer a small town feel and a quirky atmosphere. Instead of congested and fast paced activities, the Empire Asparagus Festival hosts a "Green Parade" in which no motorized vehicles are used. This festival is just about as relaxed as the quiet town itself. Situated right on the coast of Lake Michigan, the village of Empire artfully blends itself with the surrounding natural splendor. Unlike Oceana county, Empire does not lavishly boast their success. Instead the Empire Festival focuses on the humble vegetable itself and the hardworking people that grow it. Empire has a more quaint celebration, but the asparagus, the reason for celebrating, remains the same.

The asparagus industry is a serious Michigan industry, for a not so serious vegetable. Under appreciated and unknown to much of the community, this slender green vegetable is a major source of revenue not only for the Michigan economy as a whole, but also for the local Michigan growers. This nutritious vegetable is celebrated in numerous areas within Western Michigan, and it will be for years to come, as Michiganders and non-

94

Michiganders alike enjoy the culture and the delicious taste of the local and home grown Michigan asparagus.

Works Cited

Daelemans, Kathleen. "There's Nothing Like Fresh Asparagus from Michigan." *Kathleendaelemans.com.* N.p, n.d. Web. 5 Apr. 2011.

"Facts about Michigan Asparagus Industry." *asparagus.org.* Michigan Asparagus Advisory Board, 2000. Web. 7 Apr. 2011.

Lipe, Jeanne. "Select Michigan Asparagus Promotion Celebrates Michigan's First Fresh Crop of the Growing Season." *michigan.gov.* State of Michigan, 23 May 2007. Web. 1 Apr. 2011.

"National Asparagus Festival." *nationalasparagusfestival.org.* National Asparagus Festival. 2011. Web. 8 Apr. 2011.

Ward, Susan. "The Empire Strikes Back...with Asparagus." *Journal Online* (2011): n. pag. Web. 30 May 2011.

Leslie Kuhn
Writing 150

Grand Valley Weighs in on Poor Eating Habits and Lifestyle Choices

A winding line snaked its way out the doors and into the hallway. As it slowly inched forward, a woman called out names from the front of the line. It was chaos. Crowded and chattering. This could only mean one thing. It was ten o clock, and it was Kleiner Late Night. It is a routine feeding frenzy in which herds of college freshmen storm the Kleiner marketplace in search of a hot and greasy late night snack. A late night snack may seem appetizing at first to a famished college student, but the lasting effects of these poor eating habits among Grand Valley students will ultimately prove to be less than appealing. Grand Valley State University provides a number of on campus dining options, some healthy, and some not so healthy. Despite these options, weight gain among college students is not uncommon. Students continue to make poor lifestyle and eating choices, and many times these poor habits carry on into adulthood. First year GVSU students fail to acknowledge the consequences of their lifestyle choices, and the healthy alternatives and exercise resources are not being utilized as they should be.

As a whole college students gain weight in college during their first year. On average women gain four and a half pounds, and men gain about six pounds (Fitness and Wellness Center). It is apparent that these numbers are not drastic, but it is not the numbers that are troublesome. Although, students may not gain the infamous "Freshmen 15," the eating habits that college students develop during their first years are proving to be serious issues. Poor dietary and lifestyle habits can lead to diabetes, obesity, heart problems, and much more. Students need to acknowledge these potential dangers and take action to prevent them. A Grand Valley State University senior in 2005 by the name of Charles Pirtle said that he ate greasy food almost every day. At the start of his freshman year he weighed in at 155 pounds, but by the end of his college experience he weighed 175 pounds (Broaddus). This weight gain was attributed to what he ate while dining on campus. Grand Valley's dining options are varied and students have a choice in what they put into their bodies. Steven Nizielski, adviser for the nutrition emphasis in biomedical science at Grand Valley, suggests that

Campus Dining is a "mixed bag." He says, "Healthy choices are available, but many choices are far too high in fat, saturated fat and sodium" (qtd. in Broaddus). Although some healthy choices are available, students continually make unhealthy food choices with over sized portions.

In addition to avoiding weight gain itself, students are encouraged to make healthy choices. More often than not the transition from home to college leads to poor food choices, lifestyle choices. Pirtle said, "You are used to mom and dad's cooking, but when you get to college, all you have is a meal card" (Broaddus). With this meal card students tend to spend their money on cheap and accessible junk food. It is easy to have Papa John's Pizza delivered straight to your dorm room, and for many freshmen Kleiner is not but several steps away. Andy Beachnau, Grand Valley's director of health services states, "Healthy eating is a lifestyle choice" (qtd. in Broaddus). Students are continually making poor food choices. Additionally, Barbara Brenner, a registered dietitian, said, " At home teenagers usually have balanced meals prepared for them in ways that they like" (qtd. in Yarh). Away from the familiarity of home teens opt for greasy and fatty alternatives. Student's skip breakfast, and they eat late at night, hence the popularity of Kleiner late night. Brenner comments on how many students develop the habit of late night eating. She says that stressed and tired students will not hesitate to munch on junk food and consume sugary soft drinks (Yarh). In a 2010 study by Jennifer Nisenbaum, a Grand Valley senior, she found that 59 percent of students tried to eat healthy, but a majority also had acquired unhealthy eating habits, such has regularly eating after 10 p.m (Butcher 1). These are the poor lifestyle choices that college freshmen develop and carry with them into their adult lives. As a college freshman myself, I cannot help but ask Is this the lifestyle that Grand Valley and other colleges are cultivating and why are my peers oblivious to the consequences of their eating and lifestyle choices?

Ultimately, students do have a choice. All you care to eat dining such as Fresh provide healthy choices including salads, fruits, and soups, but they are consistently countered by the pizza, burgers, french fries and desserts (Broaddus). Making the healthy choices are not always easy. Eating right is a struggle, and it will continue to be a struggle. It is easy to let go of yourself and fall victim to the lifestyles of a typical college freshman. In a personal interview with Amanda Dillard, an assistant professor of the

Grand Valley State Psychology department, she said that students make unhealthy choices for a number of reasons. Dillard commented on the lack of education, and she claims that students without knowledge of proper eating habits or nutritional information will not have the necessary skills to make healthy eating choices. Informed decisions are the best decisions, and frankly students are ill informed of their nutritional health.

Dillard also touched on the effects of peer pressure on eating habits. She suggested that teens tend to have the same eating habits as their peers. This trend is apparent to me when I see large groups of student migrating to and from Kleiner and their dorms out my dorm window. When students go to eat they do so in herds, and although this creates a sense of community, this habit can be potential harmful to a student's health. If their friends eat poorly, they too will choose to adopt unhealthy eating habits. Many students are oblivious to the dangers of poor eating and lifestyle choices, and if in fact students are aware of these dangers, many do not care. Dillard mentioned the invulnerability bias to be a main motivator in the apathy felt towards proper eating. She explained the sense of invincibility that college students feel towards their eating habits. Students think they are immune to the effects of poor eating choices, and that they need not worry about their health until later in life when it "matters." As a student, I understand the logic of "enjoy it while you are young," but students fail to acknowledge that this mentality, in regards to their eating and lifestyle choices, will catch up with them eventually.

Initiative and motivation seem to be the problem at its root. Students simply are not motivated to properly take care of their bodies. I interviewed, Natalie Philips, a current Grand Valley freshman about her eating and exercise habits. She said that she would be more motivated to eat better at the dorms if more fresh fruit was available. Additionally, Philips claimed that students choose what is most available to them, and for many freshmen living in the dorms Kleiner is the closest available dining option. I surveyed thirty college freshmen, from various living centers, about their lifestyle and eating habits. The students I surveyed commented on fact that the nearest food was the greasy food. They suggested that their lack of motivation to eat well, was fueled by the lack of fresh fruit available and the presence of unhealthy options. Subsequently, Deb Rambadt, marketing manager for Campus Dining at Grand Valley said, " We have provided more healthy options along with the ones that are clearly not healthy, and students pick the less healthy options, especially late at night" (qtd. in Butcher). Rambadt also points out that healthier options have been offered previously, but these options have proved unpopular with student customers (Butcher). Evidently, despite the presence of wholesome alternatives students lack the compulsion to eat healthy.

Increasing the availability of nutritious alternatives is obvious way to improve the students motivation. By simply presenting healthier choices and making them more accessible to the busy college student, it will greatly improve the student's eating habits. Students choose the foods that are closest and easiest to take with them, and currently these foods include hamburgers, subs, fries, and nachos provided at the Kleiner dining center. As a student myself, I rarely have time to completely sit down and enjoy my food, so I opt for an apple on the go, and many students do not have this option. The Kleiner C-Store has many healthy options, but unfortunately they are also the most expensive. Additionally, those students using the meal plan must use their debit dollars on designated combinations of meals at certain dining places. This limits the options for many students, and many times they will choose to purchase greasy meals instead of healthy snacks. If fresh fruit and healthy alternatives were made more accessible to students with a limited budget and a restricting meal plan, students would opt for those food choices as apposed to resorting back to their meal plan. According to the Grand Valley Lanthorn, 3,498 students have meal plans, but 84 percent of students feel that "dining facilities on campus act as a barrier to healthy eating" (qtd. Butcher). Meal plans should incorporate the purchase of one or two fresh fruits or wholesome snacks options per day. More students would utilize that option, knowing that they would not be using valuable debit dollars every day, and in turn less perishable food would be wasted.

As a student and a skeptic myself, I like to be aware of what I am putting in my body. If students were more knowledgeable of what food they are putting their bodies and the effects of that food, they would have more of an initiative to modify their eating habits. According to the Grand Valley Lanthorn Newspaper there is a serious lack of nutritional data. Although nutritional information is available on the Grand Valley campus dining website, how many students actually check the nutritional content on a website prior to eating? Nutritional information for dining centers such as Zoca's, Caliente, Croutons, and Kleiner are unavailable, and ingredient lists are unavailable for menu items in any of the restaurants (Butcher). Nutritional information should be made available within each dining area, and students would be better informed of their food choices. Steven Nizielski, nutrition advisor, said that making nutritional information accessible has been proven to influence consumers to make better decisions. Nizielski states, "Furthermore, for those that use this information, access to nutritional information results in individuals making more healthful choices" (qtd. Butcher). Students with this additional nutritional knowledge will be better equipped to make healthy lifestyle decisions, and they would be significantly more motivated to take caution with what they put in their bodies.

Additionally, Grand Valley can only do so much in order to promote healthy lifestyles among their students, but there are several actions that Grand Valley could take. First, Grand Valley should provide health and fitness information during freshman orientation. This would start students off on the right foot, and provide them with the tools evaluate their future dining decisions. Secondly, Grand Valley should require or offer a one credit nutritional health class in order to reinforce the information provided at the beginning of the year. Lastly, drop-in sports teams should be organized. Many students want to participate in sports, but they cannot commit to the actual teams because of time constraints or financial difficulties. Drop-in sports teams would allow students to play at set times for whoever is available. These changes would provide more opportunities for students to learn the benefits of a healthy lifestyle and the consequences of poor lifestyle choices.

Students are less concerned with the health benefits associated with healthy eating than they are with their appearances. When college age students eat well or exercise, many times it is for the benefit of their appearance. Teens and young adults are concerned with their appearances and how they are perceived by the opposite sex. Dillard states that students are motivated to eat well and exercise to improve their appearance, and said, "In order to motivate students to eat well and exercise you have to make those habits seem popular." Dillard suggested a type of intervention program in which small groups of students meet with a health advisor to display to them the negative effects of their eating choices and show them the positive results, both appearance wise and health wise, of healthy eating and exercise habits. This strategy could be more effective if done not by a health advisor but instead an older student or graduate. Students tend to listen to the advice of their peers over the advice of authority figures, and seeing an older student comment on how eating healthy is "cool" would convince younger students to reconsider their current habits. If students really took the time to evaluate what they are putting in their body, they would find results that should convince them to change their unhealthy habits, and this ultimately is the goal at hand.

Grand Valley has provided numerous resources in order to help students maintain a healthy lifestyle. The solution to the poor lifestyle and eating habits lies jointly within Grand Valley and the students themselves, but Grand Valley can only do so much in order to create an incentive for a healthier life. It is the student's responsibility to take care of themselves, and it is essential that students acknowledge this and learn how to properly do so. Ultimately, the students are the ones with a choice. A choice for a better lifestyle may not be an easy one, but in the years to come students will discover the benefits of beginning healthy habits during their younger years. Healthier college students leads to healthier young professionals. If students acquire healthy eating and lifestyle habits early in life, the road to adulthood will prove to be a much smoother path.

Works Cited

Broaddus, Adrienne. "Healthy Eating Can Keep Off The Dreaded 'Freshman 15' -College Food Services Offer Well-Balanced Menu to Help Students Eat Right." *Grand Rapids Press* (14 Aug. 2005): 10. *NewsBank.* Web. 22 Feb. 2011.

Butcher, Samantha. "Eating on Campus Not As Easy As 1-2-3: Lack of Nutritional Data Creates Challenges." *Grand Valley Lanthorn*, 17 Feb. 2011, A1+. Print.

Dillard, Amanda. Personal interview. 2 Mar. 2011.

Fitness and Wellness Center. *Helpful Starts to Eating Smart: The College Student's Handbook to Better Nutrition.* Allendale, MI: Grand Valley State University, 2010. Print.

Lifestyle and Eating Habits. Survey given to GVSU freshmen. Grand Valley State University, Allendale, MI. 28 Feb. 2011.

Phillips, Natalie. Personal interview. 27 Feb. 2011.

Yarh, Emily. "How to Avoid the 'Freshman 15'; Dieticians and Students Offer Smart Strategies for Controlling Weight While Away at College." *Cleveland Jewish News* 12 Aug. 2005. *Ethnic NewsWatch.* Web. 22 Feb. 2011.

Andrew Brown
WRT 150

What's in Your Dash?

During my senior year of high school, my psychology teacher posed an interesting thought to our class. "When we die, our lives are represented by one thing: a simple, short dash sandwiched between the date of our birth and death. So what do you want your life to be; what's in your dash?" I put some thought into the one-page paper that followed, but forgot about the idea until this November.

On November 6th—over a week ago already—I was in Novi visiting my girlfriend Alex and her roommates at The Art Institute. As I was uploading some new pictures from my phone to Facebook, I was interrupted by a text from my mom. Curious, I hit "view now" and read this: "we just got home from Grand Rapids, and your grandma called. Grandpa Brown is being rushed to Lutheran Hospital; they think he had a stroke. We're on the way there right now and I'll give you more details when I know." I wasn't worried though—Grandpa was a medical marvel. Before I was born, he had a valve replaced in his heart with a pig valve that was supposed to last eight years; it never had any problems. Every month, he was forced to give blood because his body produced too much. Besides, he had survived World War II; he had to be invincible right?

An hour later, my phone rang. My mom told me that he had a major stroke on the left side of his brain, and they weren't sure of the extent of the damage yet. Because he was still listed as critical, they couldn't perform an MRI because he needed every second of care the Emergency Room could offer. She said she'd tell me more as soon as she heard it, said a choked "I love you" and hung up.

My heart plummeted to the floor as I slowly sat down right next to it. I don't remember Alex even being in the room, but somehow she was holding my head on her shoulder while I stared a hole through the wall. Shell-shocked, my brain still couldn't wrap around the idea that he was dying. He wasn't gone yet, and he had scares like this back in May and come out just fine. Two weeks earlier I had been sitting with him while he made jokes about nurses he'd had, how dumb doctors were after eight years of

Andrew wrote his portfolio in the class of Professor Michele Lussky.

school, and how nobody on this Earth could ever have as much common sense as he did. As I stared, I remembered that visit and knew I'd get to do the same thing next weekend when he got to go back home. Mostly involuntarily, my mind replayed everything I could remember about him.

Grandpa—George—was a child of the Depression. Born in 1924, getting through the impossibly difficult times required hard work, self-sufficiency, and self-reliance—it goes without saying that he also saved everything that he thought could be of importance sometime in the future. He learned to do virtually everything himself, and in the rare case he had to take something to a professional, he watched over their shoulder to learn how it was done and to correct them if they didn't do the job up to his standards. The first house my grandparents owned was built by him alone, and when they moved he poured the cement driveway, which is still smooth and unblemished today. Scattered in bags throughout the house are pictures from their many vacations, at least forty years of Christmases, and God knows how many birthdays. Surprisingly, Grandpa is in very few of them. However it wasn't that he was avoiding the camera, he was just doing what he did best: bringing happiness to the people he cared about, while standing off to the side taking none of the credit.

As with millions of other young men in the 40s, he joined the war effort in Europe. As a member of a medical battalion, he drove trucks of supplies, men, and the wounded to and from the battlefield. He walked across the sand at Normandy the day after D-Day, but never talked about the things he saw. Throughout the course of the war, he earned five Bronze Service Stars along with a myriad of smaller medals, participated in the Battle of the Bulge, and saw the horrors of a concentration camp.

A couple hours later, my phone ringer jolted me back to the present, but it was my dad this time. "Hello?"

"I love you."

"I love you too Dad, what's wrong?"

"Ok. Grandpa had a massive stroke on the left side of his brain. You probably know more about this than I do, but the doctor said that the damage is affecting his breathing, his throat…"

"His speech, the right side of his body, and depending on where it is his memory too" (I'm a Psychology major.)

Struggling through tears, he finished. "The doctors say that he most likely won't recover. The clot was at the back of his head, and cut off the blood flow to the left side. They can't take him to surgery because of his other problems, and he'd die on the table. The nurse said to let you make the decision of whether you wanted to come down and see him or not, since you're old enough to understand."

"When can you come get me?"

"Your mom will most likely come get you and your brother tomorrow afternoon. They said that any recovery will be made in the next 72 hours, so we'll just have to see. I'll see you tomorrow, I love you Andrew."

"I love you too Dad."

Click.

Alex turned and looked me in the eye: "Baby tell me." After repeating everything my dad had told me, I could barely finish as the tears started flowing. She pulled me close for a hug, and I heard her back crack at least twice as I held on for dear life, sobbing on her shoulder. We stayed that way for most of the rest of the night, my futile attempts at sleep always interrupted by memories of Christmases and birthdays from the past 19 years and keeping me awake for another hour, then another, until my phone rang again at 11 Sunday morning.

"I'm just getting ready to leave Fort Wayne, I'll let you know after I get your brother from Ann Arbor and get headed your direction. I love you Andrew."

"Ok Mom, I love you too."

Click.

I packed up my bags in slow motion, like I was watching myself from a camera in the ceiling. As my hands folded up clothes and put them back in the duffel bag, my mind was running through my grandparent's house back in Warren, remembering millions of laughs and smiles, and the time he got choked up watching us open Christmas presents. I'm not sure how many times I intentionally stubbed a toe or hit myself trying to wake up from this nightmare.

Three hours later the elevator door dinged, and I was almost tackled by my two younger sisters who were both crying. Over their shoulders I saw my Uncle Jim and Aunt Betty, who I hadn't seen in six years since Grandpa's 80th surprise party. My brother walked over and sat down almost immediately in one of the chairs, and I walked back to Grandpa's room with my dad. I sat there and talked to him while we both watched Grandpa struggle for every breath. We talked about everything, occasionally walking out to try and keep what was left of our sanity. At about 3 in the morning, we both tried to grab what sleep we could in the waiting room. After what seemed like an eternity, my mom gathered my siblings and me up so we could run down the street quick for breakfast before coming back and spending the day at the hospital.

We had just turned out on the road when Mom's phone rang. A couple "Ok's" and then "Philip turn around we need to go back." The tires squeaked as my brother whipped the car back around and put the pedal to the floor. Hospital employees stared as we raced towards Intensive Care, rushed into the elevator, and waited. A ding, the doors slid open, and we saw Dad hanging up his phone. He smiled quickly, then looked at us each in the eyes and said "he's gone." We all took turns crying on each other's shoulders, and time again moved in slow motion as we tried to console each other and grab our few belongings and leave the hospital for good. After we calmed down as much as we were going to, Dad walked Mom, my brother, and me back to the room to say goodbye. A squeeze of his hand and a choked "I love you Grandpa" was all I could manage in the eternity we seemed to be there. As my family, Grandma, and Uncle Jim and Aunt Betty walked out of the hospital, the only sound we made besides a sob was I love you.

The next few days were a blur in slow motion. The days dragged on, but when we thought about it the week was almost already over. Before any of us realized it, it was Thursday and we were on our way to visitation, then we blinked and it was Friday morning. I saw all of my cousins, who I hadn't seen since I saw Uncle Jim and Aunt Betty, six long years ago. We struggled to make it through the service, and I'm still not sure how I didn't break Alex's hand. A painful hour later, and we were sitting at the cemetery with tears running down our faces as a soldier played taps, and lost it again when the flag was folded up and handed to Grandma. Yet somehow, the thing that I still can't get out of my head really had nothing to do with Grandpa's passing at all.

After the reverend ended the service, the family stayed by the casket and exchanged long, tear-filled hugs—I even hugged my brother, who I really hadn't talked to in four months. But to truly understand the situation I have to explain my dad's family. My Uncle Jim is seventeen years older than my dad. So technically, my cousins are barely younger than my parents, and their kids are my age, and I don't honestly know what the technical term is for how we're related. Sarah, who's only a year younger than I am but technically a different generation, walked up to me and said "I haven't given you a hug yet." As we separated, she said "I wish we didn't have to see each other like this."

I've replayed that probably at least a hundred times the past few days. That one sentence made me realize the harsh reality of life: we only have so much time, and we have to make the best of what we have with the people who mean the most, friends and family. Which brings us back to the dash.

I like to picture Grandpa's dash as a semi-trailer; he drove trucks for over fifty years, including his time in the War. In it are his Army buddies, probably giving him grief about something. Covering the walls are pictures from all of the places he drove Grandma, Dad, and Uncle Jim in the RV as they saw almost everything this country has to offer. Taking up the rest of the room would be family. He impacted all of our lives so much that I'm sure we had to do the same for him. Looking back through those grocery bags full of pictures, I can tell we did, and he loved every single one of us more than any I love you could have said, which will probably still make me cry fifty years from now.

For now, I know I for sure will try and keep in better touch with family, no matter how often I see them. This short life we have just isn't long enough and is too unpredictable to make sure everyone knows how much you love them. Thank you Grandpa, for helping me see that. I'll never forget every little thing you've done for me. I love you, and miss you already.

Andrew Brown
WRT 150

Does Your Mother See Those Grades?

College football: to many a religion, or even a way of life. At the very least, it's something entertaining to watch on Saturdays, and an easy conversation topic among friends. We Americans love grilling out, getting decked out in our team's colors, and sitting down with a group of friends to watch at least one game every weekend. In the previous spring, we all saw the ten minutes of ESPN airtime dedicated to showing where the nation's top recruits had signed on to go to school in the fall. Or was it where they planned to play football in the fall? As our culture pushes the student farther out of student-athlete, these athletes are becoming more like temporary attractions for the universities they attend. They are convinced they will make it to the professional level, and they don't need to worry about what they major in or even if they graduate. Academic advisors—who are supposed to help them balance schoolwork and sports—guide them to blow-off majors and easy classes to keep them eligible. The problem with student-athletes' grades in college isn't the fault of the kids, it's in the system itself. How can we expect these kids to do well when they're set up to fail? The system of intercollegiate athletics needs to be at least revised, if not overhauled.

Doesn't the NCAA require universities to maintain certain standards of GPA, graduation rates, and other signs of academic success within the athletic department? Yes it does and the universities do adhere to them, but that isn't where the problem lies. The problem is that the universities will do anything it takes to mount a successful program. As best said by Joe Paterno, head football coach at Penn State University: "I'm not naïve. If you tell Whatsamatta U. they've got to graduate fifty percent of their kids in order to go to a bowl game, then fifty percent of the kids are going to graduate from Whatsamatta U" (Sperber). Through the actions of universities—motivated by the billion-dollar industry that is college football—unprepared student-athletes are forced into college classes, with the promises that someday they'll make it big, making the education they are supposed to be getting unimportant.

We all know vaguely how the system works: high school athletes who outperform their opponents from other high schools gain attention from college athletic departments, the student gets admitted to the college, signs a letter of intent, and goes off to school in the fall and everyone's happy. However, many athletes coming out of high school were barely eligible to play on their high school teams, leaving us wonder how the barely 2.0 student is going to the University of Michigan. This is because many institutions across the nation use a special admissions process to get those athletes admitted. This process is where a university takes an otherwise declined student, and finds some loophole to get them in, forcing—in many cases—a mediocre student at best into college-level courses. In what is becoming more prevalent, colleges are excusing poor test scores and relying on core courses in high school (Sperber). These courses are graded vastly different from school to school, which allows many athletes to earn a GPA high enough to get in via special admission. The NCAA, in trying to help students get admitted to college and get an education, is allowing students to bypass the SAT and ACT, which were created to help universities compare students from different high schools. If this continues to be allowed, the NCAA is just asking for universities and potential student-athletes to abuse it. Since there are typically more resources in high school and the classes aren't as demanding, it would be much easier for a student to earn at least decent grades, even though they may have scored very poorly on the SAT or ACT, which would reveal their true college readiness (Sperber).

This "special admission" process is widespread throughout division 1-A athletics—the highest level of athletic competition the NCAA offers—according to research done by the Atlanta Journal-Constitution (Knobler). For example, at Georgia University 73.5% of all scholarship athletes were special admittance cases, as opposed to the less than 7% in the regular student body. Wisconsin, UCLA, Clemson, Texas A&M, LSU, and Rutgers used special admissions for over half of their scholarship athletes. Nationwide, football players average 220 points lower than regular students on the SAT, with the largest gap going to the recently dominant University of Florida at 346 points. Students who don't measure up to a school's standards are "cut," denied admission. However, athletes who don't measure up academically are accepted in hopes that the school can get a slice of the multi-billion dollar industry of college athletics. As said best by Tom Lifka, director of athletic admissions at UCLA: "If you're going to mount a competitive program in Division I-A, and our institution is committed to do that, some flexibility in admissions of athletes is going to take place. Every institution I know in the country operates in the same way." Or maybe by Charles Young, former president at Florida, "We go out on the field and get beaten by people we couldn't admit. It creates strong pressures to go [to rival schools' admissions standards], and there have to be very strong countervailing pressures to avoid going there" (Knobler).

But what happens to these students when they start college? For many, an advisor sticks them in a major which is known to be easy, so the athlete can stay eligible with minimal effort. A study done by the College Student Journal examined this "academic clustering" (Schneider et al.). The study took the 12 institutions from the Big 12 Athletic Conference, all of which are known for their traditions in athletics as well as academics. The researchers recorded the majors of between thirty and fifty student-athletes from each university, and calculated the percentages of football players in each major over three seasons—1996, 2001, and 2006—and compared it to the average of regular students in that major to see if football players were being pushed towards specific majors. Not surprisingly, the study found evidence of clustering in all twelve schools in at least one of the seasons. The percentages don't appear to be that high; for example, at the University of Colorado in 1996, 30.6 % of the football players majored in sociology. However, when compared to the regular student body, it was found that only 1.5% of undergraduate students had a major in sociology. Across the conference, similar results were found in majors such as social sciences, communications, or business. This data could have just occurred by chance you say? The statistical test the researchers used calculated a less than one percent chance of this happening at random. Using the three different seasons, the researchers also took the year-by-year variance out of the equation (Schneider et al.).

Don't colleges look at their programs to ensure this doesn't happen? Surely something like this would scar an institution's good name not only amongst its athletics, but also its academics. At the University of Wisconsin, the administration conducted research of their own departments to make sure that clustering athletes into easier programs wasn't happening

(Weier). The study specifically targeted the number of athletes in direct study classes, which are one on one with a professor, and usually result in A's and B's. As far as the athletes are concerned, the class is usually an easy, high grade which can help them stay eligible, plus it has a lighter work load to compliment the amount of time athletes put into their sport. Despite the reputation of the programs, the administration found nothing wrong. They said that even though the programs typically give the good grades athletes need, they aren't the same as "blow-off" majors that other universities have. They also stated that their athletes are still capable of succeeding in the classroom, because only athletes who are capable of handling the college workload are admitted to Wisconsin. According to Professor Dresang, who works in Wisconsin's political science department, "Athletes are students like anybody else. They are good students. We do a good job of screening out athletes who will not succeed academically" (Weier).

This "review" by the school—even though it may seem like they're taking steps in the right direction—really accomplished nothing. The article stated that for one professor who had direct studies with 177 athletes, he gave 117 A's (Weier). If athletes can be advised to take a "class" and have an almost 70% chance of receiving an A in it, why wouldn't they jump at the opportunity? This is the same thing that runs rampant in other division 1 athletics; Wisconsin is merely trying to say that its system has more integrity than rival schools. The article used the case of one such athlete, who came to a professor asking for an independent study. He wanted to study the incarceration of African-Americans in the Wisconsin state prison system, and his advisor told the professor that it was the first academic topic he was interested in (Weier). This athlete obviously had no interest in academics at all, yet the professor quoted in the article said that only athletes who would succeed academically are admitted to Wisconsin. At least in my opinion, a student uninterested in academic topics doesn't really care about his degree, or even graduating.

Enough about the colleges themselves, what about the NCAA? Isn't it their job to regulate grades and graduation rates and all of that stuff when it comes to athletics anyway? Yes, it is. In fact, the NCAA has a program that pays universities that have great academic track records as a reward (Wolverton). If an institution is struggling to meet the NCAA requirements for GPA and graduation, some of that money is allotted to help them. The institutions who continue to improve their academic standing will receive the third portion of the 10 million dollar pie. The NCAA hopes that this annual payout will help give incentives to the universities to improve their academic records, as well as give the added funds to the places that need it (Wolverton).

Sure, a cut of 10 million is a lot of money, and can go a long way in an athletic department. However, aren't the billions of dollars in TV time and hours in the national spotlight, along with bowl game incentives worth a lot more than that? Offering a school $100,000 isn't going to do much when they can go out and earn millions from one football game. This is an attempt by the NCAA to make itself look good, and keep the attention off of schools' poor academic and athletic records.

So if this problem reaches all the way up to the NCAA, what can we do about it? Edward Lawry addresses the issue in his article "Academic Integrity and Athletics." In his mind, there are two types of reform: the reform of the system or the reform within the system. The first option—a reform of the system—requires the elimination of all of the money that can be found in college sports. This would include TV rights, bowl game incentives, and contracts with broadcasting companies. As long as this money is just waiting to be taken, schools will resort to any means necessary to get their hands on it, including finding loopholes in the NCAA's already loose regulations.

A second option doesn't attack the wallets of the administration directly; it requires the dropping of all NCAA requirements and guidelines. This seemingly insane tactic would take away all of the sneaking around athletic departments do, and make the universities deal with whatever reputation they decided to give themselves.

Option three seems much more likely. Institutions would be required to regularly post information on the academic quality of their athletes. This would include majors, professors, grades, test scores, and courses. If this quality of information were made public, then the NCAA and others could easily see correlations between athletes and majors, and if certain faculty members give athletes higher grades than they might deserve. It would also increase the impact of reputation on the students that are looking at a prospective university to attend: the potential applicant could see if the school treated everyone equally and just how much integrity the school really had (Lawry).

Of all of these options, the third is the most realistic but still effective option. The first one has no possibility of ever becoming effective; no college will agree to a loss of income. In the second, it already seems that schools don't currently care about their reputations with the guidelines in place, so I doubt they'd care if the guidelines were removed. However if universities were required to publish their students' academic profiles, it would be much more difficult for them to loophole their way out of the dirty ways they keep athletes on the field. In Knobler's research, he had to use data from many different years, because the universities only posted the minimum information required when mandated by the NCAA, and just that small amount of information was incriminating (College Athletes). Imagine what we could find out if they had to publish all the information they could—without violating students' privacy of course—every sports season! Such reports could cause the NCAA to reform its system until athletics resembled the Ivy League: good students just out having fun playing a sport they love, without the millions of dollars at stake.

Ultimately, it will be nearly impossible for anything to be done about this issue. Until the billions of dollars in the industry can be successfully kept from the colleges, there will always be exploitation of student-athletes. Until we can institute a plan that would indirectly hurt a university's income from athletics, we can expect to keep seeing this exploitation of student-athletes. The return of integrity into college athletics and academics: now that's something to devote fall Saturdays to.

Works Cited

Knobler, Mike. "COLLEGE ATHLETES: ACADEMIC PERFORMANCE: Behind the line on grades." *Atlanta Journal-Constitution* [Atlanta, GA] 28 Dec. 2008: A1. *General OneFile*. Web. 14 Oct. 2010.

Lawry, Edward G. "Academic integrity and college athletics." *Phi Kappa Phi Forum* Fall 2005: 20+. *General OneFile*. Web. 11 Oct. 2010.

Matthews, Frank J., and Ikenna Ofobike. "Panel discusses exploitation, academic prejudice against student-athletes: Knight commission on intercollegiate athletics wrestles with solutions at Washington summit." *Diverse Issues in Higher Education* 23.1 (2006): 8. *General OneFile*. Web. 11 Oct. 2010.

Schneider, Ray G., Sally R. Ross, and Morgan Fisher. "ACADEMIC CLUSTERING AND MAJOR SELECTION OF INTERCOL-LEGIATE STUDENT-ATHLETES." *College Student Journal* 44.1 (2010): 64-70. *Academic Search Premier*. EBSCO. Web. 14 Oct. 2010.

Sperber, Murray. "When 'Academic Progress' Isn't." *Chronicle of Higher Education* 51.32 (2005): B14-B15. *Academic Search Premier*. EBSCO. Web. 11 Oct. 2010.

Weier, Anita. "Academic Rigor; Athlete's Independent Study Draw Attention but UW Officials Say Everything is OK." *The Capital Times*. The Capital Times, 1 Jan. 2008. Web. 11 Oct. 2010.

Wolverton, Brad. "NCAA Will Pay Colleges That Raise Athletes' Academic Performance." *Chronicle of Higher Education* (2005): 39. *Academic Search Premier*. EBSCO. Web. 11 Oct. 2010.

Andrew Brown
WRT 150

To Some a Game, to Others Something More

It's a fall Friday night in Saint Joseph, which can only mean one thing: high school football. Only this Friday is different. It's Saint Joe versus Lakeshore. Tonight's game is arguably one of the biggest rivalries in high school sports; two years ago a game drew twelve-thousand fans. This particular game doesn't have quite that many, but there are easily more people than the six-thousand seats the stadium offers. Hard core fans used vacation time to leave work early and lined up outside the stadium before school ended, sitting in line for almost three hours before the gates can officially open. Both St. Joe and neighboring Stevensville are covered in decorations and signs supporting their teams. Just from the atmosphere itself, there is enough electricity to light Chicago for a month.

The rivalry has been around for more than thirty years. St. Joe is a small middle to upper class city of about 15,000, while Stevensville—home to Lakeshore High School—is more of a rural community known for Southwest Michigan's best grapes and corn. Naturally, this difference spawned the stereotypes that resulted in jokes now shared by both schools during the week of the game: St. Joe has Farmer Day and Lakeshore has Prep Day. For the most part, all of this is good-natured fun supported by both school administrations; it just adds to the excitement of Friday night.

"It's just something unlike any other. I can't think of anything that means so much to both teams, schools, and communities," said a St. Joe Bears fan whom we'll call Randy. "With the games being so competitive, it really brings both communities together, and gives the schools something to be proud of." Of course, it goes without saying that he added that "it's always good to beat the farmers," that's just how the rivalry is.

The game started just an hour later, and every fan got their money's worth. Both teams fought hard in a defensive first half, and then the coaches opened up the playbooks for the second. As the teams took turns scoring, Lakeshore took the lead with only four minutes to go. The visitors' stands boomed with cheers of "why so quiet?" while the home fans shared nervous, wide-eyed glances with each other.

St. Joe got the ball back deep in their own territory and started with two quick first downs, until disaster struck. An incomplete pass and two failed rushing attempts left Coach U and the Bears staring at a long 4th down, with eleven to go to keep the hope of victory alive. During the subsequent St. Joe time out, some fans began to pack up their blankets anticipating a turnover on downs. Narrowly beating the play clock, the Bear quarterback dropped back and found his receiver, picking up thirteen and the first down. Three plays later, the Bears again took to the air and scored the game-winning touchdown, their second come-from-behind playoff win against Lakeshore in two years.

The teams shook hands, clearly showing friendships that had been forgotten over the last few hours. Following years of tradition, St. Joe players sprinted the length of the field down to the Michelle Kruse Memorial Victory Bell, followed by singing the Alma Mater and saluting the fans. Most of those fans remained standing in the bleachers, trying to soak up as much of the atmosphere as they could.

Down in the locker room, the team celebrates. As per tradition, the team sings the same song they did when I played there: an adapted version of "We Are the Titans" from the movie Remember the Titans. Once it's over, the stereo blares whatever celebration tunes the team deems appropriate, ranging from 50 Cent to Sum 41 to Owl City. Amidst the hugs, high-fives, and "did you see that play when…"'s, the sheer joy radiates up to the ceiling and out the doors. In turn, all the players don their St. Joe t-shirts and head out to celebrate with their families, girlfriends, and close friends. I stop one player—we'll call him Big Dave—and ask him what the best part of the win is, and surprisingly it wasn't beating the farmers. "Honestly I just love seeing all the fans coming to the game. There's no feeling like playing in front of this many people, and being able to take the win back to St. Joe makes us proud to be Bears."

Walking out of the locker room, about a hundred people are still celebrating. Throughout the sea of maize and blue, the players stand with parents and loved ones, talking about something that happened on the field in between bites of booster-provided pizza. Younger children stand by the locker room door, gawking at the huge athletes that walk out, usually accompanied with a high five. Amazingly, the boys sporting peewee football jerseys tap their parents and tell them which high school player plays the same position as they do. Looking around, every single face has a smile.

The next morning I had the opportunity to chat with the old man himself: Coach Elliot Uzelac. After attending Western Michigan, he's coached for Western, the University of Michigan, Navy, Colorado, Ohio State, and even the Cleveland Browns. Legendary University of Michigan coach Bo Schembechler even mentions him in his book Bo's Lasting Lessons (102). In front of the team, he seems intimidating and constantly angry, but any other time a smile rarely leaves his time-worn face, and he always takes the time to make sure others are doing well before he worries about himself. As I walk through the door to his office, I'm met with a hug and a smile, and of course he asks me about my family, school, and my opinion of the game. After about ten minutes and some reminiscing, I ask him why he's still coaching; what makes coaching at St. Joe worth it.

"Ya know, Brownie, that's a simple question. What keeps me so into coaching is the kids; the whole job's about them anyway. I always make it a point to invest all of my time into the kids, and they'll return it in respect and performance, and grow because of it. I miss things about all of the kids I've ever coached. There's just a bond there, and even though I have my own children, each of those players is one of my own. I've been everywhere from here to Yugoslavia (Coach U is never concerned with political correctness), and St. Joe has the best kids, the best parents, and the best community of anywhere I've ever been. Football is special here, and I think the success is a big part of what keeps this community proud and in touch with its schools." He leaned back in his plush leather chair, taking a glance at the wall dedicated to team pictures from his five seasons in St. Joe and smiling.

"A few years ago when we made that playoff run to the Final Four, a man came up to me in the athletic office and said he'd be at the game on Saturday, him and the rest of his family. He said that it cost him $25 for the tickets, which was all but a couple dollars of what they had to their name. He started crying and told me that the success of the team made him believe that his family could get through their tough times and get back on their feet." He paused, and took off his glasses to wipe his eyes.

"It's the things like that that keep me here in St. Joe. We have to turn people away when they want to volunteer because we already have too many. People accuse the football program of siphoning money from the school's budget, but we don't do that either. We raise over $20,000 just on our own efforts, and get less than ten percent of what we spend from the school. We only get that much money because this program means so much to the people of this community. If I didn't have that kind of support or parental help I would've retired a long time ago."

We sat and talked for a couple more hours, before he had to shoo me out for his meeting with the assistant coaches to watch the game film from the night before. As I stood up from the chair, I couldn't help but feel like I had just spent over three hours talking to one of the most misunderstood people in Berrien County. As far as the city goes, he's just the angry Old Man; the guy who coaches the team on Friday nights, yelling and throwing his hat. But to anyone who sits down and talks to him, he couldn't be more different.

The respect his players have for him is obvious. The pictures that cover the walls and desk signed by players as far back as the 70s have messages saying something close to "thanks Coach, you have changed my life, and I will never forget you." These pictures, punctuated with frames of family and friends, show how much he affects anyone who comes in contact with him. This past year, a former teammate of mine had made no plans to attend college, mainly because of finances. When Coach U found out, he walked the kid back to his office, got on the phone to his alma mater— Western Michigan—and within an hour had him an appointment to meet with an advisor the next day. Currently, he's a full-time student at Western.

Over the past five years since Coach Uzelac's arrival, the pride in St. Joe has risen dramatically. Driving through the town, maize and blue signs that say "Bear Country" decorate about every other yard. At a stop light, about half of the cars will have some form of a bumper sticker or license plate supporting St. Joe. On Friday nights, many businesses downtown are closed, with notes in the window saying "At the game, Go Bears!" A heating and cooling company offered a discount to customers using "Bear Bucks." The business gave a one-dollar discount for every point scored by the team this season; this year, the company gave a $305 discount to every customer who had work done before the winter season began. This past spring, the city passed a bond proposal that will pay for the remodeling of the high school, adding over $200 to each resident's taxes in these tough economic times. One of the top five things Bear fans brag about isn't even about sports: the high school has been graded by the state examiners a fu. letter grade higher than Lakeshore for as far back as I can remember.

Obviously, these events aren't directly caused by a football team, but the team's success has to have played a role. It has revitalized a school and a community, and brought a sense of pride back to the school system as well as the athletic teams. I've met a large number of new people in my first year here at GVSU from all corners of Michigan, but none can believe the attention football grabs in St. Joe. To say that the football craze is exclusive to St. Joe would probably be blasphemy, but in each of those communities there is a similar story line of tradition and success. Football is a special game; the things it can do for players and fans alike are more than enough evidence for that. Before judging the sport and the people who follow it, take a second and think; to some it's more than just a game.

Works Cited

Schembechler, Bo and John U. Bacon. *Bo's Lasting Lessons.* New York: Grand Central Publishing, 2007. Print.

Uzelac, Elliot. Personal interview. 2 Nov. 2010.

Megan Kuckuk
WRT 150

...ader: How my Mind Has Changed

...d yards is equal to twenty laps of the pool. The five hundred ...ongest and hardest race there is in competitive high school swim-...ning. How long would it take you to swim twenty laps? Could you even do it without stopping? It takes me exactly five minutes and thirty seconds to swim five hundred yards. Swimming this race was my life for four years in high school. My coach counted on me to swim the five hundred at every meet and I loved doing it. I could swim for hours on end without stopping at practice and when it came time to race I knew I would crush my competition without a problem. But I didn't always have this type of confidence in myself or in my ability to be a leader on the team. It took me four long years of hard work to build up to this point of having Michael Phelps-like confidence in myself.

Before joining the varsity swim team I had previously been swimming on the club swim team which was a less serious version of the high school team. During my time at the pool I would watch members of the high school team swim with wide eyes. They were extraordinarily fast; they resembled fish since their Speedo swimsuits glistened with water like scales. I wanted to be just like them so I joined the high school team my freshman year. The first day of practice rolled along and I was a nervous wreck. I was going to be swimming with my idols for the first time and I wanted to impress them. I met my new coach, his name was Coach Downs; he was around sixty years old and as fit as a race horse. Coach Downs is more dedicated to the sport of swimming than anyone else I have ever seen; because of this he can be intimidating. His favorite activity was standing on the pool deck swearing and yelling at swimmers when they messed up until his face turned red. Coach Downs used to also carry a wooden clipboard which he regularly broke in half out of anger. He once threw the broken clipboard at the ceiling, breaking the tiles. He is not a man you want to mess with and as a freshman I was terrified of him. As I put on my swim cap and goggles the first day, my legs shook before I jumped in the water behind the other freshman on the team. Throughout the practice as I would flip my turns at the wall, I could see the upperclassmen swimming in the lanes

---

Megan wrote her portfolio in the class of Professor Monica Robinson.

next to me. I was intimidated and amazed at how fast and powerful they looked compared to me. As they raced by I didn't want them to look at me and think that I was weak or slow so I tried my hardest to keep up with the other freshman in my lane. I was so self conscious of what they thought that I just wanted to fade into the background. I had nowhere to hide as I was just wearing a tight Speedo swimsuit. I thought that there was no way that I would ever be able to swim as fast as the upperclassman on the team. I just wanted to stay out of the way of Coach Downs and avoid judgment from the upperclassman so I swam quietly in the back of the lane.

A swimming lane during practice is run similar to a road on the street which cars drive on. Swimmers swim down the right side in a line, do a flip turn at the wall and swim back down the left side. The person who swims first in the lane is the leader. They set the pace and are expected to know exactly what and how much the lane is supposed to swim according to a workout written by Coach Downs. When my lane worked on distance workouts I was asked by the others to lead so that I didn't run them over while swimming because I was faster than them at distance. I hated leading the lane because there was a lot of pressure to do everything right as everyone swimming behind you followed you and repeated what you did. If the leader swam the workout wrong the whole lane followed suit. When Coach Downs saw this he would become exceedingly angry and yell at the leader. I tried to avoid leading as much as possible, preferring to take the easier route of following someone else.

One swim practice in particular I was forced by the others in my lane to lead the distance workout. It was a long set of five hundreds where the last few laps were drills. Feeling unconfident, I unwillingly pushed off and began the tedious workout. After a while I began to lose focus which caused me to forget to swim the drills at the end. Coach Downs was standing on deck and saw me swimming the workout wrong and having the other swimmers follow me, this made him extremely angry. He made me get out of the pool, stand in front of the lane and show him what a drill looked like. I lifted my trembling arms to show him but before I could, he grabbed my arms and made them move faster. He then barked, "Get in, start over and do it the right way!" On the verge of tears, I jumped back in and started immediately. I felt embarrassed because I had been singled out. I also felt guilty because the other swimmers now had to swim more because of me. This experience furthered my dislike of being a leader.

Not only was I reluctant to lead in the water, I was shy when it came to socializing with the team. Before every meet the team had parties where we ate foods with a lot of carbohydrates to store up energy for racing. We usually watched movies or sat around a bonfire. I was typically nervous to go to these parties because they were held at the upperclassman's houses. I finally got the courage to attend one, but I only talked to a select few other freshmen and stood around feeling awkward. I got nervous and flustered around the upperclassman so I didn't ever talk to them. The team decided to play truth or dare around the bonfire at this party. The house where this was held was on farm land, and the family grew corn. When it got to my turn, a senior on the team asked me "Truth or dare?" I picked dare. She said, "I dare you to walk through the corn field to the other side alone in the dark." I said, "Alright." I got out of my lawn chair and walked to the dark edge of the corn field. I felt nervous because the entire swim team was watching and waiting for me to do it. I took a deep breath, stepped into the tall corn and just started walking to the other side. I would have been scared if I had let my imagination get the better of me, but to me it was a lame dare since I knew that bad things only happened in corn fields in the movies. When I got back to the fire from my supposedly "scary" trek alone, the team was waiting for me. The surprised looks on everyone's faces showed me that they didn't expect me to do that so carelessly because I was normally pretty quiet. They were all impressed by my bold move. This event caused the entire team to change their opinion of me. I was no longer viewed as the quiet girl who swam in the back. This change of opinion was further seen at the end season dinner banquet. This is an event which all the parents attend and awards are given out. The team captains work together to make up individual awards or mock elections which they give to every swimmer on the team. I was given the award of being the team "Jack in the box." Meaning that I occasionally did or said funny things but I was usually quiet.

My experiences with swimming over the years had built me into a skilled swimmer, which caused a drastic change in my last year of high school. The first day of practice senior year Coach Downs appointed me the leader of the distance swimming lane. There were four other underclassmen he put in my lane to follow behind me. He saw potential in these swimmers to be good at distance races so he wanted them to learn from me. Initially I felt that the year was going to be awful because there was going to be pressure on me to lead and I couldn't just swim quietly in the back any more. After a few days of practice I realized that Coach Downs had enough confidence in my swimming ability to appoint me leader of the lane. So I should also have the same confidence in myself. I began to care less about others judging me and more about swimming fast. I had no reason to feel intimidated anymore because I was an upperclassman now. Swimmers younger than me looked up to me with the same admiration as I once did to the older swimmers. I realized that I needed to step up and become a leader in order to deserve the admiration and leadership title bestowed upon me.

I was now the proud leader of the distance lane. There was one freshman swimmer named Kelly in my lane, who was introverted, reserved and quiet most of the time. I often saw her being left out of conversations and activities on the team. She swam slowly in the back of my lane because she had a hard time keeping pace with the others and me. After making these observations I felt bad for Kelly. I saw much of my old self in her because she was quiet and tried to stay out of the way. I didn't want her to feel the same feeling of intimidation I once did. As the leader I felt it was my responsibility to make an extra effort to help Kelly out. Every practice I consciously attempted to make Kelly feel welcome. Before we got in the pool for practice I would ask her how school was going for her. When we went to swim meets I sat next to her on the bus. At dinner parties I talked and made jokes with her. During practice when I saw that she was slowing down and falling behind the rest of the lane I made sure to casually give her extra encouragement.

Slowly over the year I saw a change in Kelly. She participated in team activities and she was part of the daily conversation in the lane. Her swimming times improved because I encouraged and made her keep up with the workout in the lane. At the last dinner banquet my senior year I sat at a table with my parents and Kelly's parents. After the event Kelly's mother came up to me and thanked me for helping Kelly out. She said that Kelly really looked up to me and was going to miss me when I graduated. After this conversation I realized that I had made a difference as a leader.

It took four years of hard work but over the years my attitude changed about leadership. At the beginning of my swimming career I was not a leader, but as time went on I quickly gained confidence and leadership ability. As the leader of the lane I provided guidance, instruction, encouragement and discipline to the swimmers in my lane. I kept track of time leading every workout through to the end without getting yelled at by Coach Downs who I realized wasn't the Godzilla I first thought he was. My coach and I even became friends. I got the chance to get to know him better when he offered to take me and a few other seniors out to eat pizza, dropping each of us off at home afterwards. Once I got over being nervous and intimidated it was easy for me to be a leader. I no longer wanted to hide in the back. Not caring what others though I now swam with ease and confidence. At the start of practice every day I would always be the first to snap on my cap and goggles and jump into the water eager to start warm up. I loved swimming and enjoyed my leadership position. The confidence and skills that I gained over my four year swimming career were put to good use leading the distance lane. I made a difference by teaching others how to successfully swim distance races. Being a leader helped me to grow up and be confident in myself instead of following behind others.

Megan Kuckuk
WRT 150

White Head Phones and the Disconnect

It is the year 2020. Walking down the street it is silent apart from for the rush of cars going by, when looking at other pedestrians, it is seen that every one of them has little white wires hanging out of their ears. These wires lead into their pockets or other unseen places. They are walking but it appears as if they are dancing to the personalized beats pumping into their ears. None of these people can hear anything you say or anything going on in their surroundings. Follow one of these people home and the behavior of their children is easily observed. These children can't hear you either since any action they perform they multitask with the white wires in their ears. The children take the wires out of their ears but still can't fully hear because the damage incurred to their hearing over their lifespan from the white wires. Every day these children go to school by riding the bus. But the school bus is as silent as the street with the exception of the faint sound of bass drum beats. The kids on the bus don't interact with each other because there is no need to as they all have their own personalized music entertainment system in their back pockets. This damage affects both the social and physical aspects of this future generation who have become in a sense strangled by these white wires.

The people with the white wires in their ears reveal that the end the wire is connected to either an iPod or an MP3 player. In today's world according to online statistics "275 million iPods have been sold since its release in 2001. Apple Incorporated claims that the iPod is the fastest selling music player in history. The iPod has won several awards for engineering excellence as well being highly praised for its sleek design" (Cohen). The iPod is the most widely used MP3 player because of its unparalleled popularity as a must have product. Previous versions of personal listening devices included the compact disc player and the walkman. These devices are inconvenient compared to the iPod because they require the user to carry bulky tapes or CD's. Owning an iPod gives users the ability to keep their entire music library in their back pocket, something unprecedented in the past. While the attractiveness of the iPod is obvious it also creates many serious problems. Personal listening devices like the iPod have a negative impact on society because they decrease social interaction, cause people to be disconnected and negatively affect physical health by damaging hearing.

The social devastation caused by the iPod is apparent in everyday public places because iPod listeners can be seen anywhere off in their own world disconnected from their surroundings. Personal listening devices like the iPod let users tune out their surroundings, by allowing them to be wrapped in their own private MP3 cocoon. Listeners can shut out anyone who is not in their musical world, becoming deaf to what is happening in the world. Few people know more about the behavior of iPod users than Michael Bull, a specialist in the cultural impact of technology at the University of Sussex in England. He has studied the impact of the cassette based walkman players and is now studying the affect of iPods. Bull is interviewed in an article in the London Economist he says "By granting listeners control over their environment-the audible environment, at least-the iPod allows its users to escape into their own little private bubbles. When standing in line at the airport, or waiting for a late train, iPod users feel that not everything, at least, is out of their control" ("The meaning of iPod"). Personal listening devices give the listener the ability to live in an alternate world disconnected from reality. Being deaf to their physical environment can become unhealthy because the listener is not vigilant to what is going on around them. By wearing head phones listeners can remove themselves physically from where they are by not being able to hear or respond to what is happening in their surroundings. The technology of the iPod creates numbness in the listener causing them to check out of their physical environment and into their own musical world. This is a negative effect of iPods because it causes people to become disconnected with the world around them.

Being disconnected from the surrounding environment poses multiple dangers. Hearing which one of the most important senses is blocked by wearing headphones. This is dangerous in a public setting because there is vulnerability in being deaf. For example someone wearing headphones walking down the street would not be able to hear an assailant behind them intent on harming or robbing them. The iPod itself is an item of value and could alone spark a mugging or worse. IPod listeners being disconnected from their surroundings puts them at a higher risk of crime. Wearing headphones also puts the listener at risk for other types of bodily harm. Walking on the street but not being able to hear oncoming traffic could cause catastrophic accidents between pedestrians and cars. Not being able to hear any moving objects in the surrounding environment is dangerous. According to Fox news in Florida, " A woman out for jog while listening to her iPod had her legs severed by a freight train because she may not have heard it coming, according to authorities" ("Woman Jogging, Listening to iPod"). This illustrates the danger in being disconnected in an atmosphere where being alert and attentive is important. This women's iPod distracted her from her surroundings putting her safety in jeopardy. Essentially head-phones are dangerous because they enable listeners disconnect and live in their own world.

The iPod has many uses in the modern world because listeners can use their product in virtually situation. This becomes a problem when con-sumers choose listening to their iPod over socialization in everyday life. It is no longer necessary to interact with people in public places as it is acceptable and even seen as cool to listen to an iPod and forget where you are. Every day conversations are almost impossible to have when people are plugged into their iPods in public. People with head phones on are very unapproachable, this causes decreased social interaction by closing off the outside world to the listener. This is detrimental to the social skills of our culture as a whole. A sociology professor at the University of Albany, Richard Lachmann is quoted in the Chicago Tribune saying, "Studies show that these mini-conversations, with the same woman at the coffee shop each morning or the regular banter with the guy who owns the gas station, are important to our psychological well-being. If you have a regular routine and you go back to the same places, your day can be filled with these short contacts with people you see regularly. People who don't have conversa-tions like this are really missing something" (qtd. in Leichman F01). These small conversations are extremely hard to have when people chose listen-ing to their iPod over being concerned with others around them. The iPod distracts people from their daily routine by adding music to it. This may be fun or entertaining at the present time but in the long run it prevents conversations and other important aspects of socialization. The social skills lost from using an iPod have a negative impact on society because basic so-cial skills are required in the workplace and in various other settings where communication is central to success.

The anti social behavior demonstrated in iPod users is further seen in a relatable example of the Placard Headphone Festivals which are held in London. At this event a live band plays but the audience can only listen through headphones, which they bring and plug into points at different locations. Steven Levy, the chief technology correspondent for Newsweek magazine commented on the headphone festival saying that, " The image one gets from the Headphone Festival- a live band playing to a widely scattered audience plugged into, above all, themselves, is kind of scary. What's more, is it's a perfect embodiment of the fears of the iPod critics, who see the millions of users as a digital archipelago for whom even a communal experience is transformed into a private form of aural self pleasure" (45). The headphone festival applies to the negative social effect of iPods because both cut listeners off from society. Live music which is traditionally a social event where people talk, interact and even get excited together about seeing their favorite bands had been reduce to concert goers sitting in solitude. The same thing happens to iPod listeners when they put on headphones, they make themselves isolated from others because they can't hear or respond to their surroundings.

While considering the negative social impacts there are also physical health concerns associated with the iPod. Personal listening devices can cause hearing damage through too much noise exposure. According to Dr. Rabinowitz Professor in the Department of Internal Medicine, at Yale University, hearing can be damaged by, "consistent exposure to even moderate-level loud sounds which wears out the hair cells in the inner ear that are responsible for acute hearing abilities. When these cells are damaged by noise exposure they can recover given time but with repeated exposure to loud sounds, the ability of these cells to recover weakens leading to permanent hearing loss" (2749). If iPod listeners are not careful about controlling the amount of noise they expose themselves to, it is likely they will experience varying degrees of hearing loss. An example of the damage an iPod can do is seen in an article in the Wall Street Journal, who talked to hearing specialists such as Brian Fligor, director of diagnostic audiology at Children's Hospital Boston who says, "The effects they are seeing now on iPod users hearing may be only the beginning, because accumulated noise damage can take years before it causes noticeable problems. We're only seeing a few teenagers with hearing loss at this point. But he adds that many others may have subtle hearing loss that they have yet to recognize, and by the time they do; they'll have done substantial damage" (Spencer D1). The iPods potential to cause hearing damage in its users is extremely high considering the vast amount of time the iPod is used nowadays without consideration as to the impact this might have on hearing. Personal listening devices such as the iPod have never been used at the rate they are today at any other time in history. The effect of these devices can already be seen in teenagers with hearing loss from iPods. This trend of early hearing loss is likely expected to continue because the use of iPods is not going decrease at any point in the future.

As the popularity of the iPod grows the time people spend listening to them increases. Over time, an iPod is capable of causing hearing damage depending on the level of volume the listener sets for the iPod. A leading North American market research company, NPD group, provides retail information to consumers. According to NPD group, "at maximum volume an iPod is able to emit volumes of 115 decibels, a level that falls somewhere in between a chainsaw and a jack hammer" (Spencer D1). Listening to an iPod at this level can cause serious hearing damage because according to the United States Department of Labor OSHA, the Occupational Safety and Health Administration, "the safe exposure limit on hearing is 85 decibels" (OSHA). While most iPod listeners don't listen to their iPod at full volume every time they listen the potential for damage is always present. It is commonplace for iPod users to listen to their iPod to drown out background noise in public places to help them focus. In order to drown out the background noise the volume of the iPod must be increased when using the standard headphones that come with the iPod. This puts the listener at risk of damaging their hearing because of the increased volume. The effects of listening environments on adults using MP3 players were studied by the department of speech pathology and audiology at the University of Alberta, Canada. Their research concluded that "The majority of MP3 players are sold with the earbud style of headphones. Preferred listening levels are higher with this style of headphone compared to the over-the-ear style. Moreover, as the noise level in the environment increases, earbud users are even more susceptible to background noise and consequently increase the level of the music to overcome this. The result is an increased sound pressure level at the eardrum" (Hodgetts et al. 290-297). Listening to an iPod with the provided earbud headphones in noisy environments negatively affects hearing because at high levels the iPod can emit a level of noise that is unhealthy. Over time these high levels of noise can cause serious damage leading to temporary or permanent loss of hearing.

The gloomy future of 2020 may seem unrealistic to someone who does not use an iPod or MP3 player but go to any public place today and look around, the people with the white wires in their ears will be there. Their isolation from society will be obvious as they walk alone, rejecting any social obligation that comes their way. The iPod users need for constant entertainment outweighs their desire to be connected to society. Therefore they walk around disconnected floating in their own music video for which they have personally selected the sound track. The iPod's negative effect on the user's physical hearing grows over time. A generation of iPod users will likely have a large degree of hearing loss because of improper listening practices. Hearing is a delicate sense to possess and should not be taken for granted. The iPod generation needs to wise up to the social and physical health problems associated with using personal listening devices before it is too late and society becomes strangled by the white wires.

Works Cited

Cohen, Peter. "Apple: Millions of iPods Sold, and Counting." *Macworld*. N.p., 27 Apr. 2007. Web. 4 Dec. 2010.

Hodetts, W E., J M. Rieger, and R A. Szarko. "The effects of listening environment and earphone style on preferred listening levels of normal hearing adults using an MP3 player." *U.S National Library of Medicine* (2007): 290-97. *GVSU Summon*. Web. 24 Oct. 2010.

Leichman, Abigail. "IAlone; When you're plugged in, it's easy to shut out the rest of the world." *Chicago Tribune* 25 Feb. 2006: F01. *GVSU Summon*. Web. 3 Dec. 2010.

Levy, Steven. *The Perfect Thing How the iPod Shuffles Commerce, Culture, and Coolness*. New York: Simon and Schuster, 2006. 44-45. Print.

Rabinowitz, Peter M. "Noise-induced hearing loss." *American Family Physician* 61.9 (2000): 2749. *GVSU Summon*. Web. 7 Dec. 2010.

Spencer, Jane. "Behind the Music: IPods and Hearing Loss; Some Doctors Raise Concerns That MP3 Players May Cause Damage With Heavy Use." *Wall Street Journal* 10 Jan. 2006 [New York}, eastern ed.: D1. Web. Oct. 2010.

"The meaning of iPod." *The Economist (London)* 12 June 2004: 14. *GVSU Summon.* Web. 3 Dec. 2010.

United States. Department of Labor. Occupational Safety and Health Administration. "Noise and Hearing Conservation." OSHA, National Hearing Conservation Association, Sep. 2000. Web. 5 Dec. 2010.

"Woman Jogging, Listening to iPod Had Legs Severed When Struck By Train." *Fox News.* Fox News Network, 6 July 2007. Web. 7 Dec. 2010.

Megan Kuckuk
WRT 150

"Take Nothing but Photographs, Leave Nothing but Foot Prints"

No trespassing. This area is off limits. Caution danger ahead. Disregard these signs, continue past them, seeing them only fuels your excitement. Feeling a rush of adrenaline you move faster in anticipation of what lies ahead. Driven by this unknown your eyes widen to take in your surroundings. The building you are in is crumbled and deteriorated. Everything from the walls to the floor is gray and streaked with age. The structural integrity of the floor you stand upon is questionable and the creaking under your feet is a sign that it could collapse at any moment. The air you breathe is heavy with the stench of rotting wood and the smell of dirt. But it doesn't matter; you take a deep breath because this smell enhances your experience. You are utterly alone since this is an abandoned building that is unseen and off limits. You are an urban explorer.

By definition an urban explorer is a person "who explores restricted urban areas such as abandonments, tunnels, roofs, and drains, for a hobby. They sometimes call themselves modern historians or documentarians because they take pictures of where they go and consider it art" (Paiva 14). This definition is according to a prominent urban explorer named Troy Paiva who wrote a book called Night Vision: The Art of Urban Exploration. Troy is a member of the subculture of urban exploration which community made up of people who chose not to follow the mainstream opinion of what is beautiful and what is off limits. They find beauty in crumbling man-made structures and abandoned places containing rich history. Upon first hearing about this subculture I thought it was interesting because it differs radically from my own culture. After a simple search of the internet I found myself browsing through picture after picture taken by urban explorers who were anonymous to me. The pictures were beautiful and above all fascinating because they were taken in places I had never seen before. Furthering my research I found that anyone can be part of the urban exploration subculture as long as they have a sense curiosity and adventure. The community is made up of people from all different walks of life. There is not a specific type of person who is a stereotypical urban explorer but they all share a common interest in exploring places that are unseen by most. Urban exploration is not limited to one particular place; there are explorers in every country imaginable as these countries are full of abandoned places to explore.

When on an exploration they are frequently on a journey just to take pictures and will go to great lengths to get the perfect shot. Documenting their exploration in pictures is of great importance. Explorers find decay of uninhabited spaces to be profoundly beautiful. One urban explorer in particular named Sean Galbraith was quoted in an interview saying, he takes photographs of his adventures to, "present honest and accurate representations of what cities mean and what makes them beautiful." He finds beauty in what he calls "urban architectural decay" (qtd. in Ball 84). Sean enjoys taking pictures of old machinery found in abandoned factories. His skill in his art is seen in a photo he took in an abandoned brick factory of a piece of rusted machinery. The gargantuan gears of the machine look dangerous as if they could easily crush someone. But the age of the machine is apparent in the rust which covers every surface making it look as if it hasn't moved or functioned in years. The picture documents the history of an early industrial era in an artistic way. The common theme throughout all explorers' pictures is documentation of unseen places in a way that displays them as beautiful. The goal is to capture the beauty of history in the pictures because often times abandoned places are destined for demolition.

This urban explorer named Sean, shares his artful photographs over the internet which is where members of this subculture connect. They organize expeditions, share pictures and discoveries of new places to explore over the web. Since exploring off limits can be considered trespassing which is illegal, many people are deterred from pursuing the hobby. Consequently the internet is where fellow explorers can be found. A website called Urban Exploration Resource abbreviated UER, is the main site where explorers come together. Reading through the site I learned that "Explorers will meet in person others whom they have only spoken to over the internet. When they meet they refer to each other by their online screen names" (Urban Exploration Resource). They then go on explorations together. Members of this society are welcoming to anyone who is interested in join their adventures. This is the culture of an urban explorer.

The popularity of urban exploration has risen exponentially since members began to connect over the internet. Within the website UER there are many online forums where people discuss exploring and share pictures they have taken. In general the people on these forums have agreed upon a few unwritten rules to govern the subculture. The first rule is, "take nothing but photographs, leave nothing but foot prints" (Urban Exploration Resource). This means when exploring do not disturb your surroundings as abandoned places could contain antiques or rare objects which could easily be sold on the internet. This practice is not accepted and even condemned by other explorers because it ruins the scenes history. This leads to the second rule which is, "do not vandalize or graffiti abandoned places you discover" (Urban Exploration Resource). This goes along with the first rule of don't ruin what you find. These rules are important to sustaining the culture in the future. The goal of an exploration is not to destroy, but to appreciate and respect the surrounding environment.

When explorers decide to go on an exploration locating abandoned urban areas and getting inside can be a difficult task because it is likely that the entrances are locked, guarded or even unknown. Fortunately urban explorers are known for traveling lightly with respect to gear. In a documentary called Urban Explorers: into the Darkness, a well-known explorer who goes by the nickname "Max action" was interviewed. He said, "All that is really necessary is a flashlight, a bottle of water and a camera if desired. The more advanced explorations require more equipment. Rock climbing equipment is used to scale tall buildings and mine shafts. Hard hats are good precautions along with, respirators because abandoned places can be filled with asbestos or other harmful particles. Waiters are used in drains and sewers to keep from getting wet. Lastly two way radios make for good avenues of communication between fellow explorers" (Into the Darkness). The course of an explorer's adventure can be spontaneous when walking into the unknown so being prepared for anything is a good idea. The most prized possessions in the subculture are maps of abandoned places and underground tunnels. After talking about the gear they use, Max action says, "We have better maps of the city than cops do because we have maps of everything underground and how to get in" (Into the Darkness). Having accurate maps and good map reading skills is important in the culture because it is easy to get lost in unfamiliar places, especially when exploring underground. Being ill-equipped for an exploration could have disastrous results so thoughtful preparation is essential.

The necessity of this exploring equipment illustrates the inherent danger of urban exploration. Abandoned areas are decaying and often condemned for a reason because they are dangerous. These structures cannot be counted on as being stable or secure. Exploring such places could cause them to collapse unexpectedly. Within these abandoned places it is possible that there are health hazards like asbestos, dangerous fumes, or gases such as carbon monoxide. Exploring drains is especially dangerous because of the potential of flash floods, which would cause anyone inside the drain to likely drown. Exploring unknown area also carries the risk of encroaching on gang territory which has its own risks. Not only are there physical dangers but there are legal ones too. Entering an abandoned area can be considered trespassing or an invasion of privacy, both being against the law. According to journalist Nicole Larkin who wrote an article on urban exploration, "most exploring is illegal, as many of the sites are on private property. Getting caught can result in fines or even prison time" (A8). If an urban explorer is caught by the police charges can be filed carrying serious consequences. In general being part of the subculture of urban exploring carries dangers. But members of this community over look these dangers because it is thrilling and they put their art of photography above the danger.

Urban explorers' interests lie above ground and also below. Exploring underground man-made structures is not off limits. Underground places are very alluring to urban explorers because of the mystery and adventure involved. Common underground places which are explored are: transit tunnels for subways or underground railroads, utility tunnels, sewers and also storm drains which collect rain water. Places such as catacombs are also explored; these are underground buildings mostly found in foreign countries that are off limits to tourists. My closest personal experience to underground exploration would be eating at McDonald's and playing in the play place as a child. Crawling around in the multicolored plastic tubes was the greatest adventure a kid could have. Exploring where the tunnels would lead was suspenseful and thrilling at the same time. Urban explorers get the same rush exploring underground as a child in a play place only without the safety of plastic tunnels in a restaurant protected by a clown named Ronald McDonald. Exploring underground is risky and generally off limits but this is where the thrill comes from.

From the view point of an urban explorer adventuring underground is the "holy grail" of exploring because of the history and excitement of seeing places other people don't see. In the documentary Urban Explorers: into the Darkness, a French explorer stands outside the Eifel Tower and says "look around at all these tourists marveling at their surroundings, taking pictures to document their presence at an iconic French landmark. They would never imagine that there is a world below them underground" (Into the Darkness). Urban explorers can be considered tourists of places off limits or underground. They feel the same excitement when seeing abandoned places as a tourist would seeing the Eifel Tower for the first time. They do essentially the same activities a tourist would, taking pictures, showing them to their friends and telling stories of what happened on their adventure.

The subculture of urban explorers is made up of people who don't follow the mainstream. They find beauty in what most others do not. They are willing to risk their safety and legal standing to create art and go on an adventure. Curiosity is a feeling that everyone feels, urban explorers choose to exaggerate this emotion. They feel a sense of wonder about unknown places which drive them to explore their surroundings. It is considered an accomplishment to see a place the mainstream doesn't. The photographs they take are shared through the internet but it is up to you to decide whether or not they are beautiful. Next time you see a no trespassing sign let it fuel your curiosity as to what lies on the other side.

Works Cited

Larkin, Nicole. "Urban Explorers." *Niagara Falls Review* 10 Apr. 2004 [Ontario]: A8. *GVSU Summon*. Web. 7 Dec. 2010.

Norman, Ball. "Urban Exploration." *Canadian Consulting Engineer* 48.6 (2002): 84. *GVSU Summon*. Web. 21 Nov. 2010.

Paiva, Tory. *Night Vision: The Art of Urban Exploration*. San Francisco: Chronicle Books, 2008. 14. Print.

Urban Exploration Resource. UE Main. N.p., 23 June 2002. Web. 21 Nov. 2010.

Urban Explorers: Into the Darkness. Dir. Melody Gilbert. 2007. Netflix. 7 Dec. 2010.

Good Writing Around Campus

The main purpose of the first-year writing requirement is to prepare students for the academic and professional writing they will do after their freshman year. In this section, we highlight some quality writing completed in classes beyond WRT 150. By examining some of the other pieces that were written outside of WRT 150, you will observe a wider variety of topics, styles, and forms.

The following section contains pieces written by students in GVSU courses, some of which required WRT 150 as a prerequisite. **Trevor Commee** wrote "The Importance of Practical Experience in Learning" in Professor Valerie Peterson's course, "Critical Interpretation" (COM 202). **Rachael Nolta** composed "Older-Child Adoption: An overview of how we can make older child adoption available to everyone through education, legislation, and the use of support services" in "Liberal Studies Senior Seminar" (LIB 495) under the guidance of her professor, Phyllis Vandenberg.

As you read, think about the form and content of each piece. How do the writers organize, develop, and support their essays? How have these writers learned to manipulate purpose and focus to convey information in an informative and meaningful way to their academic audience?

Trevor Commee
COM 202

The Importance of Practical Experience in Learning

Have you ever noticed the decline in the overall intelligence of people? Ever asked yourself, "Where is their common sense?" Or, "Who raised them?" For most of history the primary educators were parents. They taught their children important moral, ethical, and technical skills that ensured their success. Today, we live in the age where, most often, both parents are forced to work to support a family leaving little time to spend raising children. In the days before the cost of living exceeded the amount of money the breadwinner could bring home, it was fairly common for the wife to stay home with the children and raise them. Today, we cart our upcoming generation off to the baby sitter's house, the day-care center, or for those privileged enough, a hired nanny. If parents divorce, the children are even more likely to only have one caregiver at a time. Without the parent's direct connection to their children, it is especially challenging to pass on family traditions and to instill good character traits. In Talks to Teachers, William James highlights the importance parents have in the acquisition of learned thought and behavior. He states, "Our education means, in short, little more than a mass of possibilities of reaction, acquired at home, at school, or in the training of affairs. The teacher's task is that of supervising the acquiring process" (James 42). It is my fear that the duty of those responsible most for teaching our children, parents, are frequently absent. At the same time teachers and mentors have become babysitters who keep our children out of trouble. I do not believe that the formal system of education is broken, because it still serves several important functions. However, America is falling behind other countries in the area of intellect, and we can no longer assume that simply dropping off our children in kindergarten will result in producing perfectly formed citizens thirteen years later. It is every parent's hope that their children will become well rounded, educated, contributing members of society, and it is the primary responsibility of education to ensure that is the outcome.

Parents have the responsibility to provide an informal education (organic, individualized) to their children as to supplement what is learned in the formal system (systematic, public/private, group). In most cases, parents have the best intentions for their children; however it is not always the case for those in charge of care-taking. A babysitter does not necessarily have the same interest in making sure a child is taught important moral and ethical behavior. Babysitter's responsibilities usually include making sure a child remains in one piece (when it comes time for the parents to pick them up), ensuring they are not a danger to other children, making a point of seeing they are properly nourished, and providing other basic essentials. I am not claiming that every babysitter fits this description, but if being a babysitter is anything like any other job, and if the babysitter isn't a close friend or family member, it is hard to imagine the babysitter feeling a deep connection to a job that pays only slightly above minimum wage. Consequently, to believe the sitter is going to provide the same quality of care as a parent is hopeful, perhaps foolish.

I feel lucky that I had a family willing to devote the time and effort to raising me. I did spend some time at the daycare as a kid, but for the most part, between my grandparents, mother, father, and close family friends, I nearly always had a closely related adult mentor providing me with one-on-one interaction. My mother told me she always enjoyed seeing the world through my eyes; like it was the first time she saw the things that dazzled me. My mother took care coming down to a basic level of understanding while explaining the wonders of the world. Whether it was describing the animals at the zoo, or the rules of behavior at the super market, it took patience, time and most importantly persistence to ensure I understood. James wrote, "You may take a horse to the water, but you cannot make him drink; and so you may take a child to the schoolroom, but you cannot make him learn the new things you wish to impart, except by soliciting him in the first instance by something which naively makes him react" (James 42). My mother's knowledge of everything that went through my mind was instrumental in her teaching, because she more-or-less witnessed my entire uptake of information. Because she knew what concepts I already understood, she was able to easily relate new concepts to the old. With children, it is not lecturing which enriches the mind, it is "material things, things that move, living things, human actions and accounts of human action, [which] will win the attention better than anything that is more abstract" (James 47). Children are not interested in things like math and punctuation because they can not easily apply the knowledge to the world. My mother never tried to force me to learn anything that I was not interested in (other than how to spell my name before kindergarten); she taught me using things that were of interest and appealed to me, such as toy cars, my fish tank, weekend trips, and the endless new situations that fill our world. It is important to provide children with every opportunity to succeed. James advises to,

Crowd on the athletic opportunities, the mental arithmetic, the verse-learning, the drawing, the botany, or what not, the moment you have to reason to think the hour is ripe. The hour may not last long, and while it continues you may safely let all the child's other occupations take a second place. In this way you economize time and deepen skill; for many an infant prodigy, artistic or mathematical, has a flowing epoch of but a few months (James 55).

It is important to remember that children are not computers that can be programmed, benchmarked, or otherwise forced to learn. Parents have the unique ability to recognize when a child is about to blossom, and that opportunity should not be taken lightly.

In a school setting this type of insight does not exists, purely because it is impossible to know the experiences of every child in the classroom, let-alone just one of the students. It is important for parents to take the time to interact with their children, because they have a strong advantage when it comes to teaching. Parents have the advantage in their child's learning from the start because, they have something that teachers do not have: the love of the child. "The teacher who succeeds in getting herself loved by the pupils will obtain results which one of a more forbidding temperament finds impossible to secure" (James 46). People learn their best when they are in a healthy, stimulated frame of mind, which exists when the child is aiming to please those whom they love. In addition to James' view on the importance of love in learning, Dreyfus explains, "Unless the trainee stays emotionally involved and accepts the joy of a job well done, as well as the remorse of mistakes, he or she will not develop further, and will eventu-ally burn out trying to keep track of all the features and aspects, rules and maxims..." (Dreyfus 80).

The child working to earn or keep the admiration of a teacher is much more likely to engage the material and is willing to work harder than a child who fears punishment for not behaving or doing well. For example, in two classrooms, one with a teacher who loves their students and one where the teacher dislikes or is indifferent to students, learning will occur, but the quality of learning may not be the same. The drive to avoid punishment is strong in humans, but the desire to please those we love is even more powerful. If we see a loved one doing something, we have the impulse to imitate the behavior. "Imitation shades imperceptibly into Emulation. Emulation is the impulse to imitate what you see another doing, in order not to appear inferior" (James 48). If children love their parents, but the parents do not have the time to spend teaching their child, a second best has to be substituted (being a babysitter or a teacher at school). It takes time and effort to earn first the trust of a child, then to earn their love. In the job description for a teacher, I doubt it states: "In order to be a successful teacher, you must show compassion to your students and earn their love." Teaching is a job for many people, just like any other job. Luckily, however, most people who choose to become teacher are compassionate and do care about the betterment of students. We are lucky to have people dedicated to improving our society one person at a time.

In the classroom, in order to teach a new concept, "The instruction process begins with the instructor decomposing the task environment into context-free features that the beginner can recognize without the desired skill. The beginner is then given rules for determining actions on the basis of these features..." (Dreyfus 33). Because instructors often do not know what is already known and understood by their students, teachers have to break processes down into the most basic elements and start everybody at the same point. Although, there may be other ways of explaining the new concepts being taught, in the terms of already understood information, the teacher may not know what example(s) would bring the topic home for every student in the classroom. In an effort to prevent confusion, the teacher must break it down further. Each student has different life experiences that has constituted to their current understanding of the world. In addition to the difference in life experiences, teachers need to take in account biological differences that exist between students. For example, boys may want to read at a later age than girls do. If we separated the boys from girls, who is to say they would not perform better in developing skills (intellectual or technical). If the boys are in their prime for playing outside and climbing trees, it is going to be hard to get their mind out of the tree tops and get them to focus on long-division. Without understanding those experiences and differences, the teacher's only option is to teach to the average student, or to, by luck, notice an action that spikes an interest and then attempt to cultivate that interest into a teaching opportunity. There is simply not a low enough teacher-to-student ratio in the formal system of education.

We can not hold teachers to the same level of expectations as we do parents in instilling strong character traits such as good manners, language use, social behavior, technical skills, etc. In the upper levels of education students have the opportunity to choose teachers who are not dead to their students, but in elementary and secondary education students are often left with little options in determining whom teaches them. Teachers can only do so much, and parents need to take charge of their children's upbringing instead of simply pawning off the responsibilities to others.

The formal system of education has its purposes. The public school system is a great chance for kids to be around other children of their same age, therefore developing important social skills that will carry them throughout life. It also provides multiple viewpoints and experiences that a student otherwise would not have in a home learning environment. The school hires individuals who are specialized in one topic, and provide a diverse expertise ranging from shop class, to mathematics, to physical education. Unless at home there are super-parents, it is hard to cover so many subjects. The schoolroom is a structured environment for acquiring technical skills and to explore the different possibilities that exist for later employment and also to socialize the student. In order to move to what Dreyfus describes as competency, the students needs to feel "...the possibility of taking the risk of proposing and defending an idea and finding out whether it fails or flies" (Dreyfus 81). Without the presence of a qualified teacher it is hard to learn anything in depth. As soon as the student passes the beginning stages of learning, a mentor is needed to explain, correct, and cultivate the student to be something greater than they could on their own.

Society needs to understand learning and education is more than simply knowing facts about history, functions to solve an equation, or the understanding bodily processes. Other principals are equally important. Learning how to treat others, being courageous, respecting your elders, etc are all important life lessons that are not taught in school and require supplements from multiple facets (school, home, the grocery store, etc) to ensure the primary responsibility of education is carried out. After all, it is the hope of most parents that their child will blossom into a well rounded, educated, contributing member of society.

Works Cited

Dreyfus, Hubert. *On the Internet.* London and New York: Routledge, 2001.

James, William. T*alks To Teachers on Psychology: and to Students on some of Life's Ideals.* New York: W. W. Norton & Company Inc, 1958.

Rachael Nolta
LIB 495

Older-Child Adoption

An overview of how we can make older child adoption available to everyone through education, legislation, and the use of support services

In 2008, it was estimated that 463,000 children were in the foster care system.[1] Only 24 percent of them were residing in relative homes while 47 percent were with non-relative foster families.[2] Most of these children (52 percent) returned to their families, sadly though 48 percent of those children remained in foster care awaiting families and services.[3] Each of the children that remain in foster care have a goal for reunification with their families, adoption or some other similar goal. For those whose goal is adoption, the number of adoptive families is far fewer than the number of available children. This discrepancy leaves thousands of children without permanent and stable families, ultimately hindering their development and quality of life.

Adoption, especially older child adoption, has long been thought of as possible for only a small number of exceptionally gifted parents. These parents, it has been believed, have something "special" which allows them to be able to parent a child that is not biologically theirs or one that is suffering the consequences of a broken childhood. We often hear people say, "It isn't for everyone." But why not? Adoption, especially adoption of older children, does not have to fit into this characterization. Any parents can be incredible adoptive parents; it does not take someone "special." The first step to making older child adoption (or any adoption) a possibility for everyone is education; education about the process, education about the risks and rewards, and education about how to best parent such a child. Throughout the following pages, we will examine the foster care

---

1. Child Welfare Information Gateway. (2010). Foster care statistics. Retrieved from www.childwelfare.gov/pubs/factsheets/foster.cfm#three.
2. Child Welfare Information Gateway. (2010).
3. Child Welfare Information Gateway. (2010).

and adoption systems in Michigan, and some legislation and policies that have shaped the program. Then we will explore some of the basic social and physical effects of older child adoption. Lastly, we will try to identify the qualities necessary to become a successful adoptive parent to determine whether adoption of older children could really be a viable option for anyone.

So we begin with an overview of adoption. According to legislation and the Legal Information Institute at Cornell University Law School, adoption is the process of making an adult the legal guardian of a child thereby gaining the rights and responsibilities for them.[4] The adoptee then becomes the heir of the adopter for all legal purposes and terminates any legal relationship with their biological parents.[5] There are several different kinds of adoption one can pursue. In the broadest sense there are open and closed adoptions. Open adoptions take place when the birth mom actually selects the adoptive parents and sometimes even retains visiting rights (this is also known as a direct placement adoption[6]).[7] A closed adoption happens when the birth mom allows the state or an adoption agency to select the new parents for her child.[8] The State of Michigan Department of Human Services describes even more specific forms of adoptions like infant, agency (much like a closed adoption), relative, step-parent, intercountry or interstate, adult adoption, and state and court ward adoption.[9] Children adopted from the state have been placed into the foster care system for a variety of reasons. State and court ward adoptions are of particular interest because these children, who are often minorities, older (non-infants), in family groups, and/or have special emotional, physical or mental needs,

---

4. Legal Information Institute. (2010). Adoption. Retrieved from htt://
   topics.law.cornell.edu/wex/Adoption.
5. Legal Information Institute. (2010).
6. Michigan Department of Human Services, Adoption Services. (n.d.a).
   Adopting a child in Michigan. Retrieved from http://www.michigan.
   gov/documents/dhs/DHS-PUB-0823_221566_7.pdf.
7. Legal Information Institute. (2010).
8. Legal Information Institute. (2010).
9. Michigan Department of Human Services, Adoption Services. (n.d.a).

are the least likely to be adopted.[10] It is these children who struggle to find adoptive homes that can provide safety, stability, and structure. Next, we must look at the legal process of adoption.

The right to adopt is not guaranteed by the Constitution.[11] Instead, several statutes have been enacted to allow individuals to adopt children. Because it is not a fundamental right, adoptive parents can be deemed "unacceptable" and can legally be denied the right to adopt. The statutes regulating adoption have established this as an issue for the states to develop and regulate, however as in many cases, the influence of the Federal government can be seen in the state's policies. The Legal Information Institute at Cornell explains that Congress uses its spending power to shape the states adoption programs by granting them money to run their programs if they abide by Congress's mandates.[12] For example, the U.S. Department of Health and Human Services has established a division through the Children's Bureau and the Administration on Children, Youth and Families called the Child Welfare Information Gateway, which provides pertinent information for families, professionals, and even the state governments regarding child welfare issues including foster care and adoption. The policies initiated by this agency do not have to be followed by the states, but many chose to abide by them since they usually benefit the children and provide additional funding for the states. As a result, there are a set of federally mandated laws that permeate across the country and some adoption and foster care legislation unique to Michigan. Michigan adoption laws include policies outlining when parental consent can be given to terminate parental rights (anytime after birth at a scheduled hearing), the birth mother's expenses that can be paid for by the adoptive parents (medical, legal, counseling, reasonable living expenses for six weeks post partum, so long as all are approved by the court), and Putative father registry.[13] With a putative father registry, the alleged or reputed father of a child born out of wedlock must be notified of any proceedings to terminate parental

---

10. Michigan Department of Human Services, Adoption Services. (n.d.a).

11. Legal Information Institute. (2010).

12. Legal Information Institute. (2010).

13. Adoptive Families Magazine. (2004). Adoption laws by state. Retrieved from http://www.adoptivefamilies.com/adoptionlaws.

rights.[14] In Michigan, both mother and father must terminate parental rights. Other adoption legislation lays out the systematic process of adoption, which includes a request to adopt, an investigation and termination of the biological parent's rights among other things.

Unfamiliarity with the process and laws associated with adoption can cause many to shy away from it. Another deterrent is the cost. According to Bethany Christian Services, a leading independent adoption agency, a typical domestic infant adoption costs their organization about $20,000-$30,000 to deliver the services. Of that cost, about $11,500-$26,500 is passed on to the adoptive parents (the rest is covered by donations and partnerships). For a domestic older child adoption, Bethany's cost to deliver services is $0-$10,000 and a typical family pays $0-$3,000.[15] Obviously, there is a huge cost difference because of the incentives offered to those who chose foster care adoption but all adoptive parents cost can be lowered even further. The government, both federal and state offer tax credits for adoption. The Federal Adoption Tax Credit will cover approved adoption costs (adoption fees, court costs, attorney fees, and travel expenses) of up to $13,170 while the Michigan Qualified Adoption Expenses Credit will cover up to $1,200 for a total tax credit incentive of $14,370.[16] Many companies also offer benefits for adoptive parents of up to $10,000 (which is tax deductable) and adoption grants can provide another $4,000. With all of this assistance, the cost of a domestic infant adoption is reduced to $0-$3,500 (with just tax credits in Michigan it will cost about $5,630-$15,630) while domestic older child adoption is free.[17]

Having a basic understanding of the Michigan adoption system and having ruled out the prohibitive cost factor, we can now look at the foster care system. The Code of Federal Regulations defines foster care as a

---

14. Adoption.com. (2011). Putative fathers. Retrieved from laws.adoption. com/statutes/putative-fathers-2.html.

15. Bethany Christian Services. (2011). Financing adoption. Retrieved from http://www.bethany.org/A55798/bethanyWWW.nsf/0/5BC861 840817259285256D9E0066DE24.

16. Internal Revenue Service. (2011). Topic 607-Adoption credit. Retrieved from http://www.irs.gov/taxtopics/tc607.html.

17. Bethany Christian Services. (2011).

"24-hour substitute care for children outside their own homes."[18] These children can be placed in non-relative foster family homes, relative foster family homes, emergency shelters, residential facilities, and pre-adoptive homes.[19] Children can be placed in foster care for several different reasons. Placement is often the result of abuse and neglect in their homes. At other times, children are removed because of behavioral problems in the children, or parenting problems like abandonment, illness, incarceration, AIDS, substance abuse, or even death.[20] Not only are there different reasons for placement, there are also different kinds of placement. A court ordered placement occurs when there are reports of abuse or neglect.[21] In such a case, Child Protective Services will conduct an investigation and make a decision regarding the child's future. Other children are placed in foster care by their parents in a "voluntary placement."[22] These placements typically only last a few weeks and are a result of a hospitalization, incarceration or a similar temporary situation. Accordingly, most of the children available for adoption are placed by court order. Caseworkers evaluate each child's case individually to find the best placement for the child and any siblings.

The children that most caseworkers in Michigan work with are minorities, older children, children with physical, emotional, or mental impairments, or family groups of two or more.[23] When deciding a placement plan for children, DHS has to take into account a variety of factors. The first priority of the foster care program is to keep the children safe while also

18. Child Welfare Information Gateway. (2010).

19. Child Welfare Information Gateway. (2010).

20. American Academy of Child and Adolescent Psychiatry (2006). Facts for families: Foster care.   Retrieved from http://www.aacap.org/galleries/FactsForFamilies/64_foster_care.pdf.

21. Michigan Department of Human Services. (n.d) Children's foster care placement types and placement criteria. Retrieved from http://www.michigan.gov/dhs/0,1607,7-124-5452_7117_7658-   14897--,00.html.

22. Michigan Department of Human Services (n.d.)

23. Michigan Department of Human Services, Adoption Services. (n.d.).

listening to the child's needs.[24] They work diligently to preserve families whenever possible; they only remove the children when the family is absent or unwilling/unable to provide the child a "minimally acceptable family life" even with assistance from the state.[25] The primary purpose of the program though is to provide some consistency and permanency for the child.

Foster care placements, even for a short period, and the reasons for placement can cause trauma and other problems for the children involved. According to the American Academy of Child and Adolescent Psychiatry, foster care children struggle with feelings of guilt regarding the removal, a desire to return to birth parents, even when they were abusive, feeling unwanted and helpless, and uncertainty about the future, which often leads them to have a difficult time attaching to their foster families.[26] John and Jean Pardeck describe a series of stages children go through while they are adapting to foster care and again when adapting to an adoption placement.[27] In the first stage, children think their situation is a mistake. They may experience a loss of appetite, nightmares and other problems as a result the shock of separation from their birth parents. At the next stage, the children may be angry and protest to try to irritate their foster parents to initiate their return home. Following anger is sadness. At this stage, foster children may become sad and mope around, seemingly wanting to be comforted yet resisting. Finally, the child reaches a stage of adjustment even though they may not be entirely healed from the incident. While these stages happen for many children, it is impossible to predict how each individual child will react to a situation. Likewise, it is impossible to identify all of the potential struggles the child will have. As was mentioned, many children have trouble coping with the trauma of abuse and neglect. Others

---

24. Michigan Department of Human Services. (2006). Michigan department of human services child welfare philosophy. Retrieved from http://www.michigan.gov/documents/DHS-Child-Welfare-Philosophy_167533_7.pdf.

25. Michigan Department of Human Services. (2006).

26. American Academy of Child & Adolescent Psychiatry. (2005).

27. Pardeck, J. T. & Pardeck, J. A. (1998). Children in foster care and adoption: A guide to bibliotherapy. Westport, Connecticut: Greenwood Press.

struggle simply from being placed in a setting where the family dynamics are different from their biological family's. For instance, they may have been raised in a home with an authoritarian parent who dictated the child's every move. If that child is placed in a home where the parents are more relaxed and let the child explore, they may take longer to adjust and be more hesitant to join the new family.

While many of the risk factors associated with older child adoption vary for each child, Reactive Attachment Disorder is one of the more common risk factors associated with older child adoption. Reactive Attachment Disorder is characterized by a difficulty forming positive relationships with caregivers.[28] Forming healthy attachments with caregivers is pivotal to children's psychological development. The ease of these attachments is often dependent on whether a positive attachment was formed in the biological home and the number of placements in which the child has been put. The occurrence of this disorder increases with multiple placements and when the child is separated from their siblings. The Child Welfare Information Gateway encourages caseworkers and agencies to maintain sibling relationships as much as possible. Sibling relationships can lessen the risk of Reactive Attachment Disorder by providing the child with a consistent person in their life with which to form an attachment. The Child Welfare Information Gateway explains that, "secure attachment to an older sibling can diminish the impact of adverse circumstances such as parental mental illness or loss."[29] In the event that a sibling group cannot be kept together, professionals make every effort to enable the siblings to have visitation times. Retaining these bonds can be exponentially valuable for the child's psychological development and progress in their new home.

Not only do agencies and caseworkers work to lessen the risk factors associated with older child adoptions, the government has passed several laws to aid in this process too. While there have been several more policies passed, three of importance are the Adoption and Safe families Act of

---

28. Troutman, B., Ryan, S., & Cardi, M. (n.d.). The effects of foster care placement on young children's mental health. Retrieved from http://www.medicine.uiowa.edu/icmh/archives/reports/Foster_care.pdf.

29. Child Welfare Information Gateway. (2006a).

1997, the Children's Health Act of 2000, and the Fostering Connections to Success and Increasing Adoptions Act of 2008. The Adoption and Safe Families Act of 1997 promoted adoption as a permanency plan for more children in foster care.[30] The act proposed a program called Concurrent Planning where agencies would work to reunite the child with their biological parents while also taking steps toward another solution.[31] The goal is to put the child into the care of foster parents who would adopt the child if reunification with biological parents were not possible. This kind of program lessens the number of placements the child has to go into ultimately lessening the possibility of Reactive Attachment Disorder. Next, the Children's Health Act of 2000 made more funding available to find families to adopt children with special needs in the foster care program.[32] Lastly, the Fostering Connections to Success and Increasing Adoptions Act of 2008 made more funding available to serve the children in foster care and the new adoptive families by providing more services to make placements more successful.[33] Each of these laws have significantly influenced the workings of the foster care system and have worked to lessen the trauma that foster care children face.

Now that we have a basic understanding of the foster care system and some of the risk factors, we can start to evaluate the dynamics of families who adopt older children. Parents of older adopted children face struggles, some of which are unique, others not so unique, that have to be considered when deciding to adopt. In many cases, there is a disconnection between the parent's strengths and the needs of the child.[34] While this can be unique to adoptive families, it is also very common with biological families. For instance, it is not unusual to hear stories of athletic parents struggling to cope with raising unathletic children. While this is not exactly the same,

---

30. Child Welfare Information Gateway. (2011). Laws related to adoption. Retrieved from http://www.childwelfare.gov/adoption/laws/.
31. Child Welfare Information Gateway. (2011).
32. Child Welfare Information Gateway. (2011).
33. Child Welfare Information Gateway. (2011).
34. Ward, M. (1997). Family paradigms and older-child adoption: A proposal for matching parents' strengths to children's needs. Family Relations, 46(3), 257-262.

it illustrates how common this problem can be in any family. Another struggle is dealing with unmet or unrealistic expectations of the adoption. Many parents adopt with the idea that they will be able to swoop in, rescue the child from their life of hardship and live happily ever aver. Unfortunately, adoptive parents, like biological parents, never have such an easy parenting experience and coping with the loss of that fairy tale can prove troublesome to any parent. Another problem, more unique to adoptive parents, is coping with infertility, though it is probably best for both parent and child if this coping is completed before the adoption takes place. Lastly, adoptive parents struggle to deal with what Linda Katz calls "parental narcissism."[35] This is the notion that we feel a sense of pride in having created a human life; "the essence of parental love is a primitive sense of gratification of one's own normal narcissism."[36] To feel this gratification we look for features in infants that resemble ourselves, we see the baby as perfect. Katz goes on to explain that "this existential experience of parenthood is first a sensory and motoric experience, before it is an intellectual" one.[37] For adoptive parents of older children though, parenting is immediately an intellectual experience without having first been a sensory experience. In other words, parents must not only learn to be good parents immediately but also to love their children without having had the experience of a cooing, innocent infant. For some, this can be difficult to overcome, but it is certainly not impossible.

Another interesting aspect of parenting older child adoptees is the marital relationship between the parents. Margaret Ward conducted interviews with several different adoptive parents to see how their marriage was affected by the adoption.[38] Surprisingly, all of the changes that occurred in their marriage were things that occur in most marriages when children, biological or not, become part of the picture. The parents described a

---

35. Katz, L. (1986). Parental stress and factors for success in older-child adoption. Child Welfare, 65(6), 569-578.
36. Katz. (1986). (p.571).
37. Katz. (1986). (p. 571).
38. Ward, M. (1996). Older-child adoption and the new parents' marriage: Interviews with parents. Retrieved from http://www.eric.ed.gov/ERICWebPortal/search/detailmini.jsp?_nfpb=true&_&ERICExtSearch_SearchValue_0=ED418803&ERICExtSearch_SearchType_0=no&accno=ED418803

series of changes to the family system after the child came. For example, the needs and behaviors of the new child had to be accommodated and their emotional needs needed to be dealt with. In addition, they said the children found and exploited the family vulnerabilities and used divide and conquer strategies to achieve their desired outcome. Interestingly, the same needs must be met and the same tactics are used by biological children with their parents. Moreover, these parents described the time devoted to parent as a strain on their marriage, leaving them less opportunity to maintain their relationship. One parent said, "Adopting an older child resulted in a new balance in the partner relationship, especially for those who had no previous children in their home."[39] These same parents, however, did not identify the time spent on counseling or other similar services as a straining demand. Another parent summed up the experience by saying,

> I think that the thing that was so overwhelming from the start, which I still would say is one of the more overwhelming things now, is the constancy of it. No matter what happens to you and the rest of your life, you still have those three kids that you have to deal with when you come home. So that was the biggest thing that kind of hit me— like they're still here.[40]

If we were to ask any new parent these same questions, we would find strikingly similar responses. In all, the descriptions of the parents did not differ from what one might assume biological parents would report. Being aware of that can help us to see how similar these two parenting situations actually are.

The next and one of the most important, aspects of older child adoptions that can really encourage those who had never considered it as a parenting option are the traits that make a successful adoptive parent. As with most of what we have already looked at, these traits are not much if any different from the traits that make a successful parent of a biological child, which is encouraging for those who still believe it takes someone "special" to adopt a child. Linda Katz describes nine different traits that make a successful parent. The first, "tolerance for one's own ambivalence

39. Ward. (1996). (p.19).
40. Ward. (1996). (p. 13).

and/or strong negative feelings."[41] This just means not judging oneself for negative feelings and accepting their child's past in order to help the parent to cope with uncomfortable or unpleasant feelings. Katz suggests using humor to diffuse a difficult situation. Next is the ability to refuse rejection and to delay personal gratification. Katz says,

> Successful adoptors are stubborn, above else, and see the child's be-havior for what it is, a desperate fear of the needed closeness. When they know it has nothing whatever to do with them as people they can shrug off rejection and proceed with nurturance they know the child needs.[42]

In case the connection is not clear, biological parents are forced to do this daily, especially with teenagers. For instance, when parenting a teen-ager, parents often have to make decisions about what events the child can attend. If the parent makes an unpopular decision to best suit the long-term interests of the child, the child might "hate" them for a while. In this case, the parent is delaying their gratification and praise as a parent to best care for their child; the same happens with older child adoption. Moving forward, it is essential for parents to find happiness in small improvements. Katz also encourages parents to use flexibility in their parenting roles. This allows one parent to have a break in certain tasks while the other takes over to avoid burn out. Katz explains, "One factor distinguishing successful adoptors of older children was the ability of fathers to perceive the signs of burnout in their wives and to move into a caretaking role for the children while the wives recovered."[43] Having this supportive relationship in both biological and adoptive families can lead to a more successful home life.

Katz also encourages parents to view the family as a system. Instead of blaming one person for a problem, successful parents view each member of the family as adding something to the problem. She says, "With a systems viewpoint, the family can work toward changes in parents' behavior, sibling roles, family priorities, and so forth, as a way of handling family members'

---

41. Katz. (1986). (p.574).
42. Katz. (1986). (p.575).
43. Katz. (1986). (p. 575).

reactions to the disturbed child."[44]   Moreover, Katz describes successful parents as having a sense of entitlement as a parent. This can be encouraged by providing the parent with as much history about the child as possible. Subsequently, successful parents are intrusive and controlling. Katz explains parents should "do what parents of infants and toddlers do; they are active with the child—they assume control, try to anticipate behaviors, interrupt behavior spirals early, provide a great deal of praise, positive reinforcement, and physical affection."[45] The same is true for the success of a parent of a biological child. Successful parents are also described as using "humor and self-care," meaning they find aspects of the experience funny and they take time to recover by doing things they enjoy. Lastly, is having an open family that seeks help when it is needed and shares their troubles and stresses.

The last aspect of parenting an adoptive child that can make this a viable option for anyone is the knowledge and use of support services. Some families seek assistance from professionals who can deal with issues of loss and grief, understanding adoption, trust and attachment, school problems, post-institutionalized issues and behaviors, identity formation, birth relative contact, medical concerns, and racial issues.[46] Other services that can be helpful for adoptive and biological parents are parent support groups, online support groups, psychological therapy/counseling, respite care, seminars/conferences, books/magazines, camps and recreational activities. The use of these services can make the child's adjustment to their new family much smoother. Most importantly though, the use of these services can make adoption a possibility for anyone by providing them with the necessary resources to make the best decisions for the new child and their family as a whole.

Adoption, especially older child adoption, is often a scary choice for couples thinking about starting a family. Many couples rule this out as an option because of the risks and costs associated with adoption and the

---

44. Katz. (1986). (p. 576).
45. Katz. (1986). (p. 576).
46. Child Welfare Information Gateway. (2006b). Postadoption services. Retrieved from http://www.childwelfare.gov/pubs/f_postadoption. cfm.

uncertainty of the process. It is because of this that nearly 50 percent of the children in foster care remain there. My hope is that this paper has succeeded in doing a few different things. First, in providing some education about the adoption process and the foster care program to alleviate some of the anxiety regarding the topic. I also hope it has outlined some of the risk factors associated with adoption while also examining some of the resources available to alleviate or reduce those concerns providing the knowledge that none of these disorders has permanently "ruined" the child. Ultimately, though, I hope this document has helped to illustrate how penetrable older child adoption is; this is not only an option for the rich or the exceptional parents. Older child adoption is much like biological parenting, it requires the same skills, it brings many of the same challenges and parents reap the same rewards. We are much more familiar with the process of becoming biological parents that we rarely fear that process like we do adoption even though our biological children could grow up to have the same "problems" as adoptees. In the end, I hope this encourages more people to consider older child adoption or any kind of adoption as a viable and exciting option for their families.

References

Adoption.com. (2011). Putative Fathers. Retrieved from laws.adoption.com/statutes/putative-fathers-2.html/.

Adoptive Families Magazine. (2004). Adoption laws by state. Retrieved from http://www.adoptivefamilies.com/adoptionlaws.

American Academy of Child and Adolescent Psychiatry (2006). Facts for families: Foster care. Retrieved from http://www.aacap.org/galleries/FactsForFamilies/64_foster_care.pdf.

Bethany Christian Services. (2011). Financing adoption. Retrieved from http://www.bethany.org/A55798/bethanyWWW.nsf/0/5BC861840817259285256D9E0066DE24.

Child Welfare Information Gateway (2006a). Sibling issues in foster care and adoption. Retrieved from www.childwelfare.gov/pubs/siblingissues/index.cfm.

Child Welfare Information Gateway (2006b). Postadoption services. Retrieved from http://www.childwelfare.gov/pubs/f_postadoption.cfm.

Child Welfare Information Gateway. (2010). Foster care statistics. Retrieved from http://www.childwelfare.gov/pubs/factsheets/foster.cfm#three.

Child Welfare Information Gateway. (2011). Laws related to adoption. Retrieved from http://www.childwelfare.gov/adoption/laws/.

Internal Revenue Service. (2011). Topic 607-Adoption credit. Retrieved from http://www.irs.gov/taxtopics/tc607.html.

Katz, L. (1986). Parental stress and factors for success in older-child adoption. Child Welfare, 65(6), 569-578.

Legal Information Institute (2010). Adoption. Retrieved from http://topics.law.cornell.edu/wex/Adoption.

Michigan Department of Human Services. (2006). Michigan department of human services child welfare philosophy. Retrieved from http://www.michigan.gov/documents/DHS-Child-Welfare-Philosophy_167533_7.pdf.

Michigan Department of Human Services, Adoption Services. (n.d). Adopting a child in Michigan. Retrieved from http://www.michigan.gov/documents/dhs/DHS-PUB-0823_221566_7.pdf.

Michigan Department of Human Services. (n.d.). Children's foster care placement types and placement criteria. Retrieved from http://www.michigan.gov/dhs/0,1607,7-124-5452_7117_7658- 14897--,00.html.

Pardeck, J. T. & Pardeck, J. A. (1998). Children in foster care and adoption: A guide to bibliotherapy. Westport, Connecticut: Greenwood Press.

Troutman, B., Ryan, S., & Cardi, M. (n.d.). The effects of foster care placement on young children's mental health. Retrieved from http://www.medicine.uiowa.edu/icmh/archives/reports/Foster_care.pdf.

Ward, M. (1996). Older-child adoption and the new parents' marriage: Interviews with parents. Retrieved from http://www.eric.ed.gov/ERICWebPortal/search/detailmini.jsp?_nfpb

=true&_&ERICExtSearch_SearchValue_0=ED418803&ERICExtSea
rch_SearchType_0 =no&accno=ED418803

Ward, M. (1997). Family paradigms and older-child adoption: A proposal
for matching parents' strengths to children's needs. Family Relations,
46(3), 257-262.

GRAND VALLEY
STATE UNIVERSITY

Department of Writing

The Department of Writing offers instruction in academic, creative, and professional writing. Academic writing courses, which are designed for all students in the university community, include first-year composition and junior-level writing. For students who choose to major in writing, the department offers emphasis areas in creative and professional writing. The department also offers a minor in writing for students wishing to enhance their writing abilities for personal or professional reasons.

Academic writing, creative writing, and professional writing all belong to the liberal arts. As disciplines, they seek to sensitize student writers to the values and practices of particular genres of writing. The overall goal is to develop in students the ability to write well in a variety of contexts. Students develop this ability by reading and analyzing models and by drafting and revising original work in a workshop setting. Academic writing explores the art of writing well in specific disciplinary contexts. Creative writing explores the art of writing literary fiction, poetry, drama, and non-fiction. Professional writing explores the art of writing nonfiction and workplace writing.

The department has 45 faculty and approximately 210 majors. Altogether we offer about 250 sections a year in academic, creative, and professional writing.

Dan Royer, Chair
Professor of Writing

Lake Ontario Hall 326
Department of Writing
Grand Valley State University
1 Campus Drive
Allendale, MI 49401-9403
616-331-3411
www.gvsu.edu/writing